ANNOUNCING THE HAVERGAL EDITION
NOW IN PREPARATION FOR PUBLICATION

The edition of *The Complete Works of Frances Ridley Havergal* has five parts:

Volume I *Behold Your King:*
 The Complete Poetical Works of Frances Ridley Havergal

Volume II *Whose I Am and Whom I Serve:*
 Prose Works of Frances Ridley Havergal

Volume III *Loving Messages for the Little Ones:*
 Works for Children by Frances Ridley Havergal

Volume IV *Love for Love: Frances Ridley Havergal:*
 Memorials, Letters and Biographical Works

Volume V *Songs of Truth and Love:*
 Music by Frances Ridley Havergal and William Henry Havergal

David L. Chalkley, Editor   Dr. Glen T. Wegge, Music Editor

The Music of Frances Ridley Havergal by Glen T. Wegge, Ph.D.

This Companion Volume to the Havergal edition is a valuable presentation of F.R.H.'s extant scores. Except for a very few of her hymntunes published in hymnbooks, most or nearly all of F.R.H.'s scores have been very little—if any at all—seen, or even known of, for nearly a century. What a valuable body of music has been unknown for so long and is now made available to many. Dr. Wegge completed his Ph.D. in Music Theory at Indiana University at Bloomington, and his diligence and thoroughness in this volume are obvious. First an analysis of F.R.H.'s compositions is given, an essay that both addresses the most advanced musicians and also reaches those who are untrained in music; then all the extant scores that have been found are newly typeset, with complete texts for each score and extensive indices at the end of the book. This volume presents F.R.H.'s music in newly typeset scores diligently prepared by Dr. Wegge, and Volume V of the Havergal edition presents the scores in facsimile, the original 19th century scores. (The essay—a dissertation—analysing her scores is given the same both in this Companion Volume and in Volume V of the Havergal edition.)

 Dr. Wegge is also preparing all of these scores for publication in performance folio editions.

Frances Ridley Havergal (1836–1879). Solomon Cole painted this portrait in 1845, when she was eight years old.

Streamlets of Song
For the Young.

BY

Frances Ridley Havergal.

Collected by Her Sister,

J. Miriam Crane.

AND ALSO OTHER POEMS FOR THE YOUNG.

"Knowing her intense desire that Christ should be magnified, whether by her life or in her death, may it be to His glory that in these pages she, being dead, 'Yet speaketh!'"

Taken from the Edition of *The Complete Works of Frances Ridley Havergal*.

David L. Chalkley, Editor   Dr. Glen T. Wegge, Associate Editor

ISBN 978-1-937236-21-2   Library of Congress: 2011919010

Copyright © 2011 Frances Ridley Havergal Trust. All rights are reserved. Frances Ridley Havergal Trust P.O.Box 649 Kirksville, Missouri 63501

Book cover by Sherry Goodwin and David Carter.

CONTENTS.

PAGE

Streamlets of Song for the Young 1
Note: The list of poems and page numbers for *Streamlets of Song for the Young* is given on pages 3–5 of this book.

Addenda: Other Poems for the Young.

After *Streamlets of Song for the Young*, there are further poems by Frances and by others, listed next.

Sixteen Further Poems by F.R.H.

Arithmetical Enigma	113
Charade No. 18 (A bright and joyous frame of mind) . .	115
Say, is not my whole a prize	115
F.R.H.'s Thanks (for a pencil-case from her Bible-class) . .	117
F.R.H.'s Thanks (to Clara Overton)	118
Inscription in a Copy of "Life's Morning"	118
The Disappointed Carol Singers	118
Welcome to Winterdyne	119
To Jericho and Back	120
My Nest	125
One Question, Many Answers	125
Making Poetry	127
My Name	130
A Song of Welcome	132
"The Lord is gracious"	133
A mother's loss! Oh who may tell	136

Thirteen Poems by William Henry Havergal.

The Holy Child	139
Acrostic on the name David Clement	140
Double Acrostic on J. H. Shaw	140
For Miss Sarah Stenning	140
To John Hall Shaw	141

To Miss Caroline Kingscote	.141
Good Night	.142
Good Morning	.142
Grace before and after Meat	.142
Grace before Meat	.143
Grace after Meat	.143
To Ellen, on her Third Birthday	.143
For Evelyn, Constance, and John Crane	.144

Eight Poems by Others.

Dear child ! thy mother hath not (by Miss Threlfall)	.146
Mark 10:14 When Jesus dwelt upon this earth (by unnamed poet)	147
Hymn I am but a little child (by unnamed poet)	.147
A little dialogue Francie ! can you tell me why (by unnamed poet)	148
I'm a little pilgrim	.149
To little children There is a dove that from the glorious land (by Emma Tasham)	.149
Lord, look upon a little child (by unnamed poet)	.152
A Lesson of Trust (by Richard Wilton)	.153

LIST OF ILLUSTRATIONS.

PAGE

Frances Ridley Havergal, oil portrait painted by Solomon Cole in 1845.	ii
Jane Miriam Crane, oil portrait painted by Solomon Cole in 1845	vi
Fair copy autograph of "Love for Love" by F.R.H.	vii
F.R.H., photograph portrait, February 1, 1879.	viii
Fair copy autograph, first page, of "The Song of a Summer Stream"	6
Fair copy autograph of the "Arithmetical Enigma" in F.R.H.'s Manuscript Book Nº IV	88
Another fair copy autograph of the "Arithmetical Enigma".	.113
F.R.H., photograph portrait, undated	.116
Another photograph of F.R.H., undated	.134
F.R.H.'s manuscript of "Who will take of care of me?"	.135
F.R.H.'s manuscript of "A mother's loss"	.137
Hymn No. 569 in *Songs of Grace and Glory*, "Jesus, I will trust Thee"	138
"A Little Dialogue" and "I'm a little pilgrim" copied by hand in *The Christian Almanack for the Year 1842*	.145
Fair copy autograph of "Singing for Jesus" by F.R.H.	.154

Jane Miriam (Havergal) Crane (1817–1898), F.R.H.'s oldest sister.

Wayside Chimes. May.

Love for love.

"We have known & believed the love that God hath to us." I John 4.16

Knowing that the God on high,
 With a tender Father's grace,
Waits to hear your faintest cry,
 Waits to show a Father's face,—
Stay & think! oh should not you
Love this gracious Father too?

Knowing Christ was crucified,—
 Knowing that He loves you now
Just as much as when He died
 With the thorns upon His brow,—
Stay & think! oh should not you
Love this blessed Saviour too?

Knowing that a Spirit strives
 With your weary, wandering heart,
Who would change the restless lives,
 Pure & perfect peace impart,—
Stay & think! oh should not you
Love this loving Spirit too?

                Frances Ridley Havergal

F.R.H.'s manuscript of "Love for Love." This poem is found on page 51 of this book.

Frances Ridley Havergal, photographed in London on February 1, 1879, seven weeks after her 42nd birthday.

Streamlets of Song
For the Young.

By

Frances Ridley Havergal.

Collected by Her Sister,

J. Miriam Crane.

LONDON:
JAMES NISBET & CO., 21 BERNERS STREET.
1887.

Preface

In the happy days that have passed away, I asked my dear sister, Frances Ridley Havergal, to make up a volume of her most simple poems for the dear little ones growing up around us. She at once promised to do so, but from the many claims on her time was never able to carry out the idea.

I have therefore now made a selection, and believe that these "Streamlets of Song" will afford pleasure and profit to many young readers. Pure and sparkling as the mountain rills, or calm and reviving as the brooks of the valley, they tend to show how the lambs of the flock may be invigorated on the hills of God, or be refreshed in the green pastures of spiritual teaching, while still enjoying the innocent playfulness of childhood, and the bright imaginings of youth.

J. Miriam Crane

Weston-super-Mare.

[Miriam (Jane Miriam Havergal Crane) was F.R.H.'s oldest sister, and she knew her very well her entire life. Miriam leaves us wanting more from her and more about her. She wrote the biography of their father, *Records of the Life of the Rev. William Henry Havergal, M.A.*, she edited Frances' *Swiss Letters and Alpine Poems* and Maria V. G. Havergal's *Autobiography*, and she compiled and published *Streamlets of Song for the Young*. Nineteen when Frances was born, Miriam began to tutor her youngest sister when she was two and a half: a small card written in Miriam's hand clearly states in category by category her young student's progress in the subjects. Miriam taught Frances poetry, helping to begin, nourish, develop, the rare gift which later was used so richly and beneficially, and there is a handwritten manuscript volume of many poems by contemporary and earlier poets which (apparently) Miriam and Frances copied and studied. She was the first born of her parents' six children, and she was the last to die, living 19 years beyond Frances' death (1817–1898). Edited by her and published by Nisbet in 1887, *Streamlets of Song for the Young* is especially noteworthy because of Miriam's place in Frances' life.]

Contents

TITLE	DATE	WHERE WRITTEN	PAGE
The Song of a Summer Stream	Feb. 18, 1879,	Caswell Bay	7
Flowers	Oct. 16, 1869,	...	8
My Little Tree	Oct. 22, 1869,	...	9
The Bower	Oct. 21, 1869,	...	10
The Moon	Oct. 21, 1869,	...	10
Stars	Oct. 18, 1869,	...	11
Who will take Care of Me?	Jan. 1, 1873,	...	12
Trust	Oct. 23, 1869,	...	13
Sunday Bells	Oct. 18, 1869,	...	13
A Prayer	1849,		14
Prayer before Church	1849,		15
Evening Prayer	Oct. 17, 1869,	...	15
Thy Kingdom Come	Oct. 22, 1869,	...	16
Auntie's Lessons	Nov., 1865,	Oakhampton in Astley	16
Ethelbert's "Coming Home in the Dark"	July 27, 1874,	Towyn	17
Loving Messages	1878,	...	20
The Dying Sister	Oct. 23, 1869,	Towyn	21
Begin at Once!	May, 1876,	...	22
A Happy New Year	1874,	Winterdyne	23
New Year Hymn	1872,	...	24
Candlemas Day	Feb. 1, 1869,	...	25
May Day	1851,	Leamington	26
The Dawn of May	May 13, 1855,	Oakhampton	27
Ascension Song	Dec., 1871,	...	28
The Happiest Christmas Day	1872,	Perry Barr	29
The Angels' Song	Oct. 24, 1869,	...	30
Christmas Sunshine	Dec. 25, 1878,	...	31
Birthday Mottoes	1877,	...	34
M. L. C.'s Birthday Crown	July 11, 1859,	Oakhampton	37
John H. C.'s Third Birthday	Nov. 27, 1858,	...	37
Coming of Age	Sept. 26, 1865,	Celbridge	39
The Children's Triumph	Mar. 29, 1873,	Perry Barr	39
Coming into the Shade	Oct., 1875,	Upton Bishop	40
The Sunday Book	Oct. 5, 1872,	Oakhampton	42
Baby's Turn	1869,	Worcester	43
For Charity	Sept., 1874,	Ormont Dessous	44

TITLE	DATE	WHERE WRITTEN	PAGE
Severn Song	1873,	...	44
My Mother's Request	Feb. 6, 1854,	...	45
At Home To-night	Dec. 19, 1872,	Perry Barr	47
An Indian Flag	1873,	...	49
Love for Love	Feb. 12, 1879,	Caswell Bay	51
The Turned Lesson	Mar. 28, 1876,	Leamington	51
My Singing Lesson	Nov. 26, 1867,	London	53
Leaning over the Waterfall	May, 1874,	...	55
"That's not the Way at Sea"	1876,	Leamington	56
The Awakening	1874,	...	57
Something to Do	Feb. 12, 1877,	...	59
Little Nora	Dec., 1856,	...	64
"Come Over and Help Us"	1856,	...	67
The English Child's Reply	1856,	...	68
A Plea for the Little Ones	April 2, 1872,	...	69
Two Rings	1870,	...	73
The Mountain Maidens	July, 1873,	Switzerland	77

ANSWERS TO ENIGMAS.

No. 1. Needles	89
No. 2. Lines	89
No. 3. Table	90
No. 4. Trunk	91
No. 5. Sere, Seir, seer, sear (seared)	92
No. 6. Malice	92
No. 7. Scrape, Crape, Ape	93
No. 8. Bacon	93
No. 9. Lava	94
No. 10. Ball	94
No. 11. Box	95
No. 12. Spring	96
No. 13. Lock	97
No. 14. Pole	97
No. 15. Ice	98
No. 16. Gas	100
No. 17. Shadow	100
No. 18. Arch	101
No. 19. Melodies	102
No. 20. A Riddle	103
No. 21. Wheels	103

CONTENTS.

Answers to Charades.

	PAGE
No. 1. Cutlass	104
No. 2. Carpet	104
No. 3. Orion	105
No. 4. Ivanhoe	105
No. 5. Iceland	106
No. 6. Hemlock	107
No. 7. Wordsworth	108
No. 8. Harebell	108
No. 9. Parsonage	108
No. 10. Palmerston	109
No. 11. Larkspur	110
No. 12. Nightingale	110
No. 13. Sunday	110
No. 14. Bargain	111
No. 15. Gentleman	111
No. 16. Rampart	112
No. 17. Dande(y)lion	112

After *Streamlets of Song for the Young*, these are further poems by Frances.

TITLE	DATE	WHERE WRITTEN	PAGE
Arithmetical Enigma		...	113
F.R.H.'s Thanks (for a pencil-case from her Bible-class)	Mar. 23, 1858,	...	117
F.R.H.'s Thanks (to Clara Overton)	1871,	...	118
Inscription in a Copy of "Life's Morning"	1861,	...	118
The Disappointed Carol Singers	1855,	...	118
Welcome to Winterdyne	Dec. 15, 1866,	Oakhampton	119
To Jericho and Back	Dec., 1868,	Winterdyne	120
My Nest	Aug., 1869,	...	125
One Question, Many Answers	April, 1857,	...	125
Making Poetry	Jan., 1868,	...	127
My Name	April 1, 1868,	...	130
A Song of Welcome	Nov. 22, 1857,	...	132
The Lord Is Gracious	1858,	...	133
A mother's loss! Oh, who may tell	1852,	...	136

After *Streamlets of Song for the Young*, there are further poems by Frances and by others, the list with page numbers for those given on pages iv–v of this book.

41

The Song of a Summer Stream

A few months ago
I was singing through the snow
Though the dead brown boughs gave no
~~sign~~ hope of summer shoots,
And my persevering fall
Seemed to be no use at all,
For the hard, hard frost would not let me
reach the roots.

Then the mists hung chill
All along the wooded hill,
And the cold sad fog through my lonely
dingles crept;
I was glad I had no power
To awake one tender flower
To a sure, swift doom! I would rather that
it slept.

Still I sang all alone
In the sweet old summer tone
For the strong white ice could not hush
me for a day;
Though no other voice was heard

The first page of F.R.H.'s handwritten manuscript of "The Song of a Summer Stream." She copied out her poems in Manuscript Books, and this was written in her last one, which had written by her on the front page, "Manuscript Book No. IX." and then below that on the front page, "Begun Febr. 24. 1878." and then the Scripture, "'I will direct their work in truth.' Isa. 61.8."

Streamlets of Song For the Young.

The Song of a Summer Stream.

A FEW months ago
I was singing through the snow,
Though the dead brown boughs gave no hope of summer shoots,
And my persevering fall
Seemed to be no use at all,
For the hard, hard frost would not let me reach the roots.

Then the mists hung chill
All along the wooded hill,
And the cold, sad fog through my lonely dingles crept;
I was glad I had no power
To awake one tender flower
To a sure, swift doom! I would rather that it slept.

Still I sang all alone
In the sweet old summer tone,
For the strong white ice could not hush me for a day;
Though no other voice was heard
But the bitter breeze that whirred
Past the gaunt, grey trunks on its wild and angry way.

So the dim days sped,
While everything seemed dead,
And my own poor flow seemed the only living sign;
And the keen stars shone
When the freezing night came on,
From the far, far heights, all so cold and crystalline.

A few months ago
I was singing through the snow!
But now the blessed sunshine is filling all the land,

And the memories are lost
Of the winter fog and frost,
In the presence of the Summer with her full and glowing hand.

Now the woodlark comes to drink
At my cool and pearly brink,
And the ladyfern is bending to kiss my rainbow foam;
And the wild-rose buds entwine
With the dark-leaved bramble-vine,
And the centuried oak is green around the bright-eyed squirrel's home.

O the full and glad content,
That my little song is blent
With the all-melodious mingling of the choristers around!
I no longer sing alone
Through a chill surrounding moan,
For the very air is trembling with its wealth of summer sound.

Though the hope seemed long deferred,
Ere the south wind's whisper heard
Gave a promise of the passing of the weary winter days,
Yet the blessing was secure,
For the summer time was sure
When the lonely songs are gathered in the mighty choir of praise.

Flowers.

Buds and bells! Sweet April pleasures,
   Springing all around,
White and gold and crimson treasures,
   From the cold, unlovely ground!
He who gave them grace and hue
   Made the little children too!

When the weary little flowers
   Close their starry eyes,
By the dark and dewy hours
   Strength and freshness God supplies.
He who sends the gentle dew
   Cares for little children too!

Then He gives the pleasant weather,
    Sunshine warm and free,
Making all things glad together,
    Kind to them and kind to me.
Lovely flowers! He loveth you,
    And the little children too!

Though we cannot hear you singing
    Softly chiming lays,
Surely God can see you bringing
    Silent songs of wordless praise!
Hears your anthem, sweet and true,
    Hears the little children too!

My Little Tree.

THEY tell me that my little tree
Is only just my age, but see,—
Already ripe and rosy fruit
Is peeping under every shoot!
How little have I brought,
But withered leaves of foolish thought;
And angry words, like thorn,
How many have I borne!

No fruit my little tree can bring
Without the gentle rain of spring;
Nor could it ever ripen one,
Without the glowing summer sun:
O Father! shed on me
Thy Holy Spirit from above,
That I may bring to Thee
The golden fruit of love.

Let sunshine of Thy grace increase
The pleasant fruit of joy and peace,
With purple gleam of gentleness,
That most of all my home may bless;
While faith and goodness meet
In ruby ripeness rich and sweet,

Let these in me be found,
And evermore abound.

The Bower.

Will you come out and see
   My pretty bower with me,
My sweet little house that lilac boughs have made;
   With windows up on high,
   Through which I see the sky,
And look up to Him who made the pleasant shade?

   The sunbeams come and go
   So brightly to and fro,
Like angels of light, too dazzling to be seen!
   They weave a curtain fair
   About my doorway there,
And paint all my walls with shining gold and green.

   I have sweet music too,
   And lovely songs for you,
To hear in my house among the lilac leaves;
   For breezes softly play,
   And robins sing all day:
I think this is praise that God on high receives.

The Moon.

"The moon walking in brightness."—Job 31:26.

Not long ago the moon was dark,
   No light she gave or gained;
She did not look upon the sun,
   So all her glory waned.
Now through the sky so broad and high,
   In robe of shining whiteness,
Among the solemn stars of God,
   She walks in brightness.

Look up to Him who is the Sun,
    The true and Only Light,
And seek the glory of His face,
    His smile so dear and bright.
Then making gladness all around,
    By gentleness and rightness,
You, too, shall shine with light divine,
    And walk in brightness.

Stars.

THE golden glow is paling
    Between the cloudy bars;
I'm watching in the twilight
    To see the little stars.
I wish that they would sing to-night
    Their song of long ago;[1]
If we were only nearer them,
    What might we hear and know!

Are they the eyes of Angels,
    That always wake to keep
A loving watch above us,
    While we are fast asleep?
Or are they lamps that God has lit
    From His own glorious light,
To guide the little children's souls
    Whom He will call to-night?

We hardly see them twinkle
    In any summer night,
But in the winter evenings
    They sparkle clear and bright.
Is this to tell the little ones,
    So hungry, cold, and sad,
That there's a shining home for them,
    Where all is warm and glad?

---

[1] "When the morning stars sang together."—JOB 38:7.

More beautiful and glorious,
    And never cold and far,
Is He who always loves them,
    The Bright and Morning Star.
I wish those little children knew
    That holy, happy light!
Lord Jesus, shine on them, I pray,
    And make them glad to-night.

Who will take Care of Me?

Written for Emily F. W. W. Snepp.

WHO will take care of me? darling, you say!
    Lovingly, tenderly watched as you are!
Listen! I give you the answer to-day,
    ONE who is never forgetful or far!

He will take care of you! all through the day,
    Jesus is near you to keep you from ill;
Walking or resting, at lessons or play,
    Jesus is with you and watching you still.

He will take care of you! all through the night,
    Jesus, the Shepherd, His little one keeps;
Darkness to Him is the same as the light;
    He never slumbers and He never sleeps.

He will take care of you! all through the year,
    Crowning each day with His kindness and love,
Sending you blessing and shielding from fear,
    Leading you on to the bright home above.

He will take care of you! yes, to the end!
    Nothing can alter His love to His own.
Darling, be glad that you have such a Friend,
    He will not leave you one moment alone!

Trust.

Sadly bend the flowers
 In the heavy rain;
After beating showers,
 Sunbeams come again.
Little birds are silent
 All the dark night through;
When the morning dawneth,
 Their songs are sweet and new.

When a sudden sorrow
 Comes like cloud and night,
Wait for God's to-morrow;
 All will then be bright.
Only wait and trust Him
 Just a little while;
After evening tear-drops
 Shall come the morning smile.

Sunday Bells.[1]

O sweet Sabbath bells!
 A message of musical chiming
Ye bring us from God, and we know what you say;
 Now rising, now falling,
 So tunefully calling
His children to seek Him, and praise Him to-day.

The day we love best!
 The brightest and best of the seven,
The pearl of the week, and the light of our way;
 We hold it a treasure,
 And count it a pleasure,
To welcome its dawning and praise Him to-day.

---

[1] From "Sacred Songs for Little Singers," Novello & Co.

O sweet Sabbath rest!
   The gift of our Father in heaven;
A herald sent down from the home far away,
   With peace for the weary,
   And joy for the dreary:
Then, oh! let us thank Him, and praise Him to-day.

Rejoice and be glad!
   'Tis the day of our Saviour and Brother,
The Life that is risen, the Truth and the Way;
   Salvation He brought us
   When wand'ring He sought us,
With blood He hath bought us: then praise Him to-day.

A Prayer.

Lord, in mercy pardon me
All that I this day have done:
Sins of every kind 'gainst Thee,
O forgive them through Thy Son.

Make me, Jesus, like to Thee,
Gentle, holy, meek, and mild,
My transgressions pardon me,
O forgive a sinful child.

Gracious Spirit, listen Thou,
Enter in my willing heart,
Enter and possess it now,
Never, Lord, from me depart.

O eternal Three in One,
Condescend to bend Thine ear;
Help me still towards heaven to run,
Answer now my humble prayer.

Prayer before Church.

Lord, I am in Thy house of prayer,
Oh, teach me rightly how to pray;
Incline to me Thy gracious ear,
And listen, Lord, to what I say.

Give me, O Lord, a praying heart,
And also an attentive ear;
Help me to choose the better part,
And teach me Thee to love and fear.

Evening Prayer.

Now the light has gone away,
Saviour, listen while I pray,
Asking Thee to watch and keep,
And to send me quiet sleep.

Jesus, Saviour, wash away
All that has been wrong to-day,
Help me every day to be
Good and gentle, more like Thee.

Let my near and dear ones be
Always near and dear to Thee;
Oh, bring me and all I love
To Thy happy home above!

Now my evening praise I give:
Thou didst die that I might live,
All my blessings come from Thee;
Oh, how good Thou art to me!

Thou, my best and kindest Friend,
Thou wilt love me to the end!
Let me love Thee more and more,
Always better than before!

Thy Kingdom Come.

God of heaven! hear our singing;
    Only little ones are we,
Yet a great petition bringing,
    Father, now we come to Thee.

Let Thy kingdom come, we pray Thee,
    Let the world in Thee find rest;
Let all know Thee, and obey Thee,
    Loving, praising, blessing, blessed!

Let the sweet and joyful story
    Of the Saviour's wondrous love,
Wake on earth a song of glory,
    Like the angels' song above.

Father, send the glorious hour,
    Every heart be Thine alone!
For the kingdom, and the power,
    And the glory are Thine own.

Auntie's Lessons.

They said their texts, and their hymns they sang,
    On that sunny Sabbath-day;
And yet there was time ere the church-bell rang,
    So I bid them trot away.
And leave me to rest and read alone,
Where the ash-tree's shade o'er the lawn was thrown.

But oh! 'twas a cry and a pleading sore,
    "O Auntie! we will not tease,
But tell us one Sunday story more;
We will sit so still on the grassy floor;
Tell us the one you told before
    Of little black Mumu, please,
Whom, deaf and dumb, and sick and lone,
    The good ship brought to Sierra Leone."

Willie begged loud, and Francie low,
      And Alice, who could resist her?
Certainly not myself, and so
The story was just beginning, when lo!
      To the rescue came my sister.
"*I* will tell you a story to-day;
Aunt Fanny has all her own lessons to say!"

Wonderful notion, and not at all clear!
      Alfred looked quite astounded.
Who in the world *my* lessons could hear?
They guessed at every one far and near,
      'Twas a mystery unbounded.
They settled at last that it must be
Grandpapa Havergal over the sea.

Then merry eyes grew grave and wise,
      On tiptoe Alice trod;
She had a better thought than they,
And whispered low, "Does Auntie say
      Her lessons all to God?"
How little the import deep she knew
Of those baby-words, so sweet and true!

Little she knew what they enfold!—
      A treasure of happy thought;
A tiny casket of virgin gold,
      With jewels of comfort fraught.
Great men's wisdom may pass away,
Dear Alice's words in my heart will stay.

Ethelbert's "Coming Home in the Dark."

DID I tell you how we went to tea,
All by ourselves, with kind Mrs. B.?
And how we came home in the dark so late,
I think it was nearly half-past eight!
We liked the tea, and all the rest,
But coming home in the dark was best, —

Best of all! oh, it *was* such fun,
The nicest thing we have ever done.
Nurse took Willie, and Bertha took me,—
Bertha is such a great girl, you see;
She sometimes says to us, "Now, little boys,
Don't you make such a dreadful noise,
You will wake little Sybil with all your riot!"
And then we have to be—oh, so quiet!
She is nearly eight, and ever so tall;
But Willie and I are not very small;
We are six years old, and our birthdays came
Both on one day, the very same.
So people say we are little twins,
And as much alike as two little pins.
And Papa likes having a pair of boys,
Although we make such a dreadful noise;
" Much more amusing," we heard him say,
" Than a couple of odd ones any day!"
 It was only so very dark down below
Along the lane where the blackberries grow,
For the little stars were out in the sky,
And we laughed to see them, Willie and I,
For they twinkled away, so quick and bright,
I think they were laughing at us that night.
A bright one got up from behind a tree,
And peeped at Bertha and Willie and me;
And round the corner we saw another
Playing at hide-and-seek with his brother,
Popping out from a cloud, and then
Running behind it to hide again.
 And then the kind little Moon came out
To take care of the Stars as they played about;
She looked so quiet and good, we thought
That perhaps they went to her school to be taught,
And to learn from her how to shine so bright;
But Grandmamma told us we did not guess right,
For the Moon goes to school herself to the Sun:
Do you think she meant it only in fun?
 Then all of a sudden the Wind ran by,

And flew up to kiss the Stars in the sky;
He tucked them up, and said good-night,
And drew the curtain round them tight.
That was a great dark cloud, you see,
That hid the Stars from Willie and me.
I think they were sorry to go to bed,
For they did not look tired at all, we said;
And one or two of them tried to peep;
But very soon they were all asleep,
For the Wind kept singing their lullaby,
And we felt quite vexed with him, Willie and I.

   I think the Moon asked if she might not stay
To light us a little bit more of the way,
But he whistled quite loud, and we thought he said,
"No, no, no! you must go to bed!"
The good little Moon did what she was bid,
And under the curtains her pretty face hid;
And then it got darker and darker still;
Nurse said she was setting behind the hill.
So perhaps she was tired, and glad to go;
It's a long way across the sky, you know.

   We were not afraid, but we did not talk
As we came along the avenue walk;
And we did not *quite* like looking back,
For the pretty green trees were all quite black.
But I whispered to Willie that God was there,
And we need not be frightened, for He would take care

   And then all at once we saw the light
In the dining-room window, ever so bright;
And up we came through the little gate,—
Oh, it *was* so nice to come home so late!
And then we gave a famous shout,
For dear Mamma herself came out
To meet us, just as we got to the door;
But she had not expected us home before.
And then we took it by turns to talk,
And tell them about the tea and the walk;
And Papa *did* laugh so,—we wondered why!
At what we told him, Willie and I.

Loving Messages for the Little Ones.[1]

EVERY little flower that grows,
    Every little grassy blade,
Every little dewdrop, shows
    Jesus cares for all He made.
Jesus loves, and Jesus knows!
    So you need not be afraid!

FAIR the blossoms opening early!
    For the dew
Fell upon them, cool and pearly,
    Brightening every hue.
Like a little thirsty flower,
    Lift your face,
Seek the gentle, holy shower
    Of the Spirit's grace.

GRACE and glory! They are yours
    Through the Saviour's dying love;
For His own sweet word endures
    Longer than the stars above.
It shall never pass away,
So trust His living love to-day.

HAVE you not a song for Jesus?
    All the little buds and flowers,
All the merry birds and breezes,
    All the sunbeams and the showers,
Praise Him in their own sweet way!
What have you to sing to-day?
Bring your happiest songs, and sing
For your Saviour and your King.

---

[1] Six floral cards for Caswell.

KNOWING Christ was crucified,
    Knowing that He loves you now
Just as much as when He died
    With the thorns upon His brow,—
Stay and think! oh, should not you,
Love this blessèd Saviour too?

OPENING flowers I send to you
With a message sweet and true.
They may fade, but Jesus lives,—
Peace and grace and joy He gives.
Come to Him and you will know
What He waiteth to bestow!

The Dying Sister.

DARLING boy,
Sister's joy,
With your loving smile,
Kiss me now,
On my brow,
Stay with me awhile!
He who has lovèd me,
He whom I longed to see,
Calls me away;
I must not stay.

He is near,
True and dear,
Darling, do not cry!
Jesus too
Loveth you,
Loves you more than I.
Kneel by my pillow here,
Tell Him the sorrow, dear;
He is so kind,
This you will find.

Angels bright,
Robed in light,
In that happy home,
Singing wait
At the gate,
Till He bids me come.
Soon, brother, I shall see
Him who has died for me;
I am so glad,
Yet you are sad.

Hymn and prayer
We did share,
Many an evening past;
Jesus heard
Every word,
This may be the last.
Ere next the light grows dim,
I may be there with Him.
Praising Him too,
Waiting for you!

Begin at Once!

Band of Hope Song.

BEGIN at once! In the pleasant day,
  While we are all together,
While we can join in prayer and praise,
While we can meet for healthful plays,
  In the glow of summer weather.
Begin at once, with heart and hand,
And swell the ranks of our happy band.

Begin at once! For we do not know
  What may befall to-morrow!
Many a tempter, many a foe
Lieth in wait where'er you go,
  With the snare that leads to sorrow.

Begin at once! nor doubting stand,
But swell the ranks of our happy band.

Begin at once! There is much to do;
   Oh, do not wait for others!
Join us to-day!—be brave and true;
Join us to-day!—there's room for you,
   And a welcome from your brothers.
Begin at once! for the work is grand
That God has given to our happy band.

Begin at once! In the strength of God
   For that will never fail you!
Under His banner, bright and broad,
You shall be safe from fear and fraud,
   And from all that can assail you.
Begin at once,—with resolute stand,
And swell the ranks of our happy band.

A Happy New Year.

A HAPPY New Year! Oh such may it be!
Joyously, surely, and fully for thee!
Fear not and faint not, but be of good cheer,
And trustfully enter thy happy New Year!

Happy, so happy! Thy Father shall guide,
Protect thee, preserve thee, and always provide!
Onward and upward along the right way
Lovingly leading thee day by day.

Happy, so happy! Thy Saviour shall be
Ever more precious and present with thee!
Happy, so happy! His Spirit thy Guest,
Filling with glory the place of His rest.

Happy, so happy! Though shadows around
May gather and darken, they flee at the sound
Of the glorious Voice that saith, "Be of good cheer!"
Then joyously enter thy happy New Year!

New Year Hymn.

Jesus, blessèd Saviour,
    Help us now to raise
Songs of glad thanksgiving,
    Songs of holy praise.
O how kind and gracious
    Thou hast always been!
O how many blessings
    Every day has seen!
        Jesus, blessèd Saviour,
            Now our praises hear,
            For Thy grace and favour
                Crowning all the year.

Jesus, holy Saviour,
    Only Thou canst tell
How we often stumbled,
    How we often fell!
All our sins (so many!),
    Saviour, Thou dost know;
In Thy blood most precious,
    Wash us white as snow.
        Jesus, blessèd Saviour,
            Keep us in Thy fear,
            Let Thy grace and favour
                Pardon all the year.

Jesus, loving Saviour,
    Only Thou dost know
All that may befall us
    As we onward go.
So we humbly pray Thee,
    Take us by the hand,
Lead us ever upward
    To the Better Land.
        Jesus, blessèd Saviour,
            Keep us ever near,
            Let Thy grace and favour
                Shield us all the year.

Jesus, precious Saviour,
    Make us all Thine own,
Make us Thine for ever,
    Make us Thine alone.
Let each day, each moment,
    Of this glad New-year,
Be for Jesus only,
    Jesus, Saviour dear.
        Then, O blessèd Saviour,
            Never need we fear,
        For Thy grace and favour
            Crown our bright New-year!

Candlemas Day.

YES, take the greenery away
That smiled to welcome Christmas Day,
Untwine the drooping ivy spray.

The holly leaves are dusty all,
Whose glossy darkness robed the wall,
And one by one the berries fall.

Take down the yew, for with a touch
The leaflets drop, as wearied much
With light and song, unused to such.

Poor evergreens! Why proudly claim
The glory of your lovely name,
So soon meet only for the flame?

Another Christmas Day will show
Another green and scarlet glow,
A fresh array of mistletoe.

And this new beauty, arch or crown,
Will stiffen, gather dust, grow brown,
And in its turn be taken down.

To-night the walls will seem so bare!
Ah, well! look out, look up, for there
The Christmas stars are always fair.

They will be shining just as clear
Another and another year,
O'er all our darkened hemisphere.

So Christmas mirth has fleeted fast,
The songs of time can never last,
And all is buried with the past.

But Christmas love and joy and peace
Shall never fade and never cease,
Of God's goodwill the rich increase.

May Day.

O HASTE, O haste to the fields away!
    For dawneth now the month of May;
O leave the city's crowded street,
    And haste ye now sweet May to greet.

For May is come on fairy wings,
    And thousand beauties with her brings;
The fairest month of all the year,
    Oh, well can she the sad heart cheer.

Nature her jewelry displays,
    Unfolds her gems to meet our gaze;
Bright leaves and buds of *emerald* hue,
    Forget-me-nots of *sapphire* blue.

The *pearly* lily's drooping bells,
    Listen! a tale it sweetly tells:
"If God so clothe the lilies fair,
    Much more may ye trust in His care."

The *turquoise* gentianella bright,
    The shining king-cup's golden light,

Carnation's *ruby* hues behold,
   And *silvery* daisy set with *gold*.

Of these we'll twine a garland gay,
   Meet for the brow of beauteous May;
And see, they gain a brighter hue
   By glittering drops of *diamond* dew.

Now hark! what sound so sweetly floats
   Upon the breeze? The cuckoo's notes!
How far they come to welcome May,
   And pour for us the simple lay!

The Dawn of May.

COME away, come away, in the dawn of May,
   When the dew is sparkling bright;
     When the woods are seen
      All in golden green
   In the crystal, crystal light.
The sweet perfume of violet bloom,
   And hawthorn fragrance rare,
     From the cool mossy shade,
     Or the warm sunny glade,
   Is filling all the air.

Come away, come away, in the dawn of May,
   When the lark and the white cloud meet;
     When the tuneful breeze,
      In the old oak trees,
   Is harping, harping sweet.
With joyous thrill and merry trill,
   The thrush and blackbird vie,
     As they chant loving lays,
     And a full song of praise,
   To the Lord of earth and sky.

Come away, come away, in the dawn of May,
   In the pearly morning-time,

When the cowslips spring,
    And the blue-bells ring
Their fairy, fairy chime.
With happy song, we march along,
    And carol on our way,
        One in heart, one in voice,
        Let us all now rejoice
In the sunny dawn of May.

Ascension Song.

"He ascended up on high."—EPHESIANS 4:8.

GOLDEN harps are sounding,
    Angel voices ring,
Pearly gates are opened—
    Opened for the King;
Christ, the King of Glory,
    Jesus, King of Love,
Is gone up in triumph
    To His throne above.
        All His work is ended,
        Joyfully we sing,
        Jesus hath ascended!
        Glory to our King!

He who came to save us,
    He who bled and died,
Now is crowned with glory
    At His Father's side.
Never more to suffer,
    Never more to die,
Jesus, King of Glory,
    Is gone up on high.
        All His work is ended,
        Joyfully we sing,
        Jesus hath ascended!
        Glory to our King!

Praying for His children,
   In that blessèd place,
Calling them to glory,
   Sending them His grace;
His bright home preparing,
   Faithful ones, for you;
Jesus ever liveth,
   Ever loveth too.
      All His work is ended,
         Joyfully we sing,
      Jesus hath ascended!
         Glory to our King!

The Happiest Christmas Day.

SYBIL, my little one, come away,
I have a plan for Christmas Day:
Put on your hat, and trot with me,
A dear little suffering girl to see.

'Tis not very far, and there's plenty of time,
For the bells have not begun to chime;
So, Sybil, over the sparkling snow
To dear little Lizzie let us go.

Dear little Lizzie is ill and weak,
Only just able to smile and speak.
Yesterday morning I stood by her bed;
Now, shall I tell you what she said?

"Christmas is coming to-morrow," said I.
"I shall be happy!" was Lizzie's reply;
"Happy, *so* happy!" I wish you had heard
How sweetly and joyously rang that word.

"Dear little Lizzie, lying in pain,
With never a hope to be better again,
Lying so lonely, what will you do?
Why will the day be so happy to you?"

Lizzie looked up with a smile as bright
As if she were full of some new delight;
And the sweet little lips just parted to say,
"I shall think of Jesus all Christmas Day!"

How would you like to take her the spray
Of red-berried holly I gave you to-day?
And what if we gave her the pretty wreath too
That Bertha has made with ivy and yew?

The green and the scarlet would brighten the gloom
Of dear little Lizzie's shady room;
And, Sybil, I know she would like us to sing
A Christmas song of the new-born King.

Sybil, my little one, if we do,
It will help us to "think of Jesus" too;
And Lizzie was right, for that is the way
To have the happiest Christmas Day!

The Angels' Song.

Now let us sing the Angels' Song,
    That rang so sweet and clear,
When heavenly light and music fell
    On earthly eye and ear,—
To Him we sing, our Saviour King,
    Who always deigns to hear:
        "Glory to God! and peace on earth."

He came to tell the Father's love,
    His goodness, truth, and grace;
To show the brightness of His smile,
    The glory of His face;
With His own light, so full and bright,
    The shades of death to chase.
        "Glory to God! and peace on earth."

He came to bring the weary ones
    True peace and perfect rest;

To take away the guilt and sin
    Which darkened and distressed;
That great and small might hear His call,
    And all in Him be blessed.
        "Glory to God! and peace on earth."

He came to bring a glorious gift,
    "Goodwill to men";—and why?
Because He loved us, Jesus came
    For us to live and die.
Then, sweet and long, the Angels' Song
    Again we raise on high:
        "Glory to God! and peace on earth."

Christmas Sunshine.

Do the angels know the blessed day,
    And strike their harps anew?
Then may the echo of their lay
    Float sweetly down to you,
And fill your soul with Christmas song
That your heart shall echo your whole life long.

Jesus came!—and came for me!
    Simple words! and yet expressing
Depths of holy mystery,
    Depths of wondrous love and blessing.
Holy Spirit, make me see
All His coming means for me;
Take the things of Christ, I pray,
Show them to my heart to-day.

Oh, let thy heart make melody,
    And thankful songs uplift,
For Christ Himself is come to be
    Thy glorious Christmas gift.

A happy, happy Christmas,
    And a happy, happy year!
Oh, we have not deserved it,
    And yet we need not fear.
For Jesus has deserved it,
    And so, for Jesus' sake,
This cup of joy and blessing
    With grateful hand we take.

There is silence high in the midnight sky,
    And only the sufferers watch the night;
But long ago there was song and glow,
    And a message of joy from the Prince of Light,
And the Christmas song of the messenger-throng
The echoes of life shall for ever prolong.

Great is the mystery
    Of wondrous grace,
God manifest we see
    In Jesu's face.
O deepest mystery
    Of Love Divine,
God manifest for me,
    And Jesus mine!

What was the first angelic word
That the startled shepherds heard?—
"Fear not!" Beloved, it comes to you
As a Christmas message most sweet and true,
As true for you as it was for them
In the lonely fields of Bethlehem;
And as sweet to-day as it was that night,
When the glory dazzled their mortal sight.

CHRIST is come to be my Friend,
   Leading, loving to the end;
Christ is come to be my King,
   Ordering, ruling everything.
Christ is come! Enough for me,
Lonely though the pathway be.

GIVE me a song, O Lord,
   That I may sing to Thee,
In true and sweet accord
   With angel minstrelsy.
Oh, tune my heart that it may bring
A Christmas anthem to my King.

SWELL the notes of the Christmas Song!
   Sound it forth through the earth abroad!
     Glory to God!
   Blessing and honour, thanks and laud!
Take the joy of the Christmas Song!
   Are not the tidings good and true?
     Peace to you,
And God's good-will that is ever new!

CHRIST is come to be thy light,
Shining through the darkest night;
He will make thy pilgrim way
Shine unto the perfect day.
Take the message! let it be
Full of Christmas joy to thee!

Birthday Mottoes.

MAY the tale the years are telling,
    Always be
Like an angel-anthem swelling
Through thy spirit's quiet dwelling,
Till the glory all-excelling
    Dawn for thee!

MANY a happy year be thine,
    If our Father will!
He has traced the fair design,
He will fill it, line by line,
    Working patiently, until
Thy completed life shall shine,
Glorious in the life divine.

MANY and happy thy birthdays be!
    In the light of heaven arrayed;
With the rainbow arching every cloud
    When the pathway lies in shade;
And full and far may the blessing flow,
    That thy future life is made.

LOVE would strew upon thy way
    Fairest, freshest flowers to-day;
Love would daily, hourly shed
    Brightest sunbeams on thy head.
So she prays: that heavenly grace
    Be thy flower-awakening dew,
And the brightness of His face
    Gild thy life with sunshine true.

"Upward, still upward" thy pathway be,
Into the sunshine grand and free;
Leaving the mists and clouds below,
Gaining the pure and stainless snow.
Upward, still upward! Thy faithful Guide
Always close at His pilgrim's side,
Leading thee on from height to height,
Nearer and nearer the stars of light.

Birthday blessings, fullest, sweetest,
    Fall on thee to-day!
Earthly pleasure, fairest, fleetest,
    Will not, cannot stay;
But the true and heavenly treasure
    Cannot pass away :
May its richest, grandest measure
    Gild thy natal day!

The Love of God the Father,
    The Grace of God the Son,
The joy of God the Holy Ghost,—
    A blessing three in one,
Be yours aboundingly, I pray,
For this and every coming day!

Leaning, resting, trusting, loving,
    Enter thy new year!
For the Lord who lives to love thee
    Will be always near,
Shielding, guiding, caring, blessing!—
    What hast thou to fear?

We pray Thee for our dear one!
    May a sunny birthday prove
The portal of long happy years,
    All radiant with Thy love.
And we praise Thee for our dear one!
    For all the mercies past,
And for all the blessing that shall flow
    While life itself shall last.

A holy, happy birthday
    And a happy, happy year!
Ah, we have not deserved it,
    And yet we need not fear.
For Jesus has deserved it!
    And so, for Jesus' sake,
This cup of joy and blessing
    With grateful heart we take.

I have no birthday gifts to bring,
    But I will crave a Royal dower,
The sevenfold largesse of the King.

His Peace be thine, His Love unknown;
    His own deep Joy, His Strength and Power,
His Grace abounding, be thine own!

His Rest be thine, sweet rest to-day,
    Rest while the swift years pass away,
And then His Glory thine for aye!

M. L. C.'s Birthday Crown.

ONLY just a line to say,
Miriam, on this summer day,
What my spirit's love would breathe,
While thy birthday crown I wreathe.

Crown! How many a mingled thought
By that little word is brought!
Yet may each enlinkèd be
In a birthday wish for thee.

One who wears a crown should reign
Sovereign over some domain;
Held by thee, love's fairy sway
Still may every heart obey.

First we think of royal gems,
Coronets and diadems;
'Twere an idle wish, I ween,
Be thou happy as a Queen!

To another crown we turn,
While our loving hearts would burn,
Worn by Him who on the tree,
Miriam, hath died for thee.

By that thorn-enwoven crown.
By the life for thee laid down,
May thy every fleeting year
Bring thee to His love more near!

Then the crown of golden light,
Worn by those who walk in white,
May that be thy blest reward
In the presence of thy Lord!

To John Henry C— on his Third Birthday.

BLESSINGS on thee, darling boy,
Peace and love and gentle joy!

May the coronal they twine
Through the dream of life be thine!

Little hast thou known of life,
Of its sorrow, of its strife,
Thine not yet dark Future's blast,
Thine not yet a shadowy Past.

While we reck of coming years,
Strangely mingling hopes and fears,
What are sober thoughts to thee,
In the tide of birthday glee!

Thou art beautiful and bright,
Daily wakening new delight,
Would that we the prize could hold,
Always keep thee three years old!

No, not always; thou may'st be
Something brighter yet to see,
Noble-hearted, lofty-souled,
When more years have o'er thee rolled.

Love is watching round thee now,
Tracing sunbeams on thy brow;
Never be her mission done
To thy father's only son!

Yet a higher, deeper love
Watcheth o'er thee from above
Then thy fount of motive be
Love to Him who loveth thee.

Darling, may thy years below
Like a strain of music flow,
Ever sweeter, purer, higher,
Till it swell the angel choir.

Be thy life a star of light,
Glistening through earth's stormy night,
Shining then with glorious ray
Through the One Eternal Day!

"Coming of Age."

(J. H. S.)

What do we seek for him to-day, who, through such golden gates
Of mirth and gladness, enters now where life before him waits?
'Mid light and flowers the feast is spread, and young and old rejoice,
And motto texts speak out for all, with earnest, loving voice.

The threefold blessing Israel heard three thousand years ago,
Oh! grant it may on him to-day in power and fulness flow;
For, faithful and unchangeable, each word of God is sure,
Though heaven and earth shall pass away, His promises endure.

The Angel of the Covenant, redeeming from all ill
Both son and father, bless the lad, and every prayer fulfil;
Nor only bless, but make him, too, a blessing, Lord, from Thee :
With length of days, oh, satisfy; let him Thy glory see.

Through all the journey of his life, Thy presence with him go;
Rest *in* Thee here, and *with* Thee there, do Thou, O Lord, bestow.
Oh, keep him faithful unto death, then grant to him, we pray,
The crown of glory and of life, that fadeth not away.

So shall the father's soul be glad for him he holds so dear,
A son whose heart is truly wise in God's most holy fear;
And hallowed be our festal joy with gratitude and praise;
Forget not all His benefits, whose kindness crowns our days.

Then glory in the highest be to Him, our Strength and Song;
May every heart uplift its part, in blessings deep and long.
Through Him who died that we might live, our thanks to God ascend,
The King of kings, and Lord of lords, our Saviour and our Friend.

The Children's Triumph.

The Sunbeams came to my window,
    And said, "Come out and see
The sparkle on the river,
    The blossom on the tree!"

But never a moment parleyed I
    With the bright-haired Sunbeams' call!
Though their dazzling hands on the leaf they
    laid,
I drew it away to the curtain-shade,
    Where a sunbeam could not fall.

The Robins came to my window,
    And said, "Come out and sing!
Come out and join the chorus
    Of the festival of the Spring!"
But never a carol would I trill
    In the festival of May;
But I sat alone in my shadowy room,
And worked away in its quiet gloom,
    And the Robins flew away.

The Children came to my window,
    And said, "Come out and play!
Come out with us in the sunshine,
    'Tis such a glorious day!"
Then never another word I wrote,
    And my desk was put away!
When the Children called me, what could
    I do?
The Robins might fail, and the Sunbeams
    too,
But the Children won the day.

Coming into the Shade.

Out in the midsummer sunshine,
    Out in the golden light,
Merrily helping the gardener,
    Ever so busy and bright, —
With tiny barrow and rake and hoe,
Helena flitted to and fro.

But the midsummer sun rose higher
    Over the flowery spot;
"I must rest a little now," she said,
    "I am so tired and hot.
Oh, let me come to you, and look
At the pictures in your beautiful book."

Why we should leave the sunny lawn
    She did not understand,
But cheerily, trustfully, Helena laid
    In mine, her little brown hand,
And I led her away to a shady room,
To rest in the coolness and the gloom.

For she could not have seen the pictures
    Out in that dazzling light;
The book was there with its colours fair,
    But the sunshine was too bright.
But in the shade I could let her look
At the pictures in my beautiful book.

"I have never seen them before," she said,
    "I am so glad I came!
And the gardener will manage the flowers, I think
    Without me, just the same!
And I need not trouble at all, you know,
About my barrow and rake and hoe."

So page after page was gently turned,
    As I showed her one by one,
And told her what the pictures meant,
    Till the beautiful book was done.
And *then*—I shall not soon forget
The loving kiss of my tiny pet.

And *now*—I shall not soon forget
    The lesson she had taught,
How from the sunshine into the shade
    God's little ones are brought,
That they may see what He could not show
Among the flowers in the summer glow.

The Sunday Book.

READ to him, Connie, read as you sit,
    Cosy and warm in the great arm-chair,
    Let your hand press lovingly, lightly there,
    Let the gentle touch of your sunny hair
Over his cheek like a soft breeze flit.

Read to him, Connie! The house is still,
    The week-day lessons, the week-day play,
    And the week-day worries are hushed away
    In the golden calm of the Holy Day;
He will listen now if ever he will.

Read to him, Connie, read while you may!
    For the years will pass, and he must go
    Out in the cold world's treacherous flow,
    Danger and trial and evil to know,—
He may drift in the dark, far, far away!

Now he is happy and safe in the nest,
    Teach him to warble the songs of home,
    Teach him to soar but never to roam,
    Only to soar to a starry dome,
Linking with heaven the hearts he loves best.

Read to him, Connie! Read what you love,
    Holy and sweet be your Sabbath choice;
    And the music that dwells in a sister's voice
    Shall lure him to listen while angels rejoice,
As the soft tones blend with the harps above.

Read to him, Connie! Read of the ONE
    Who loves him most, yes, more than you!
    Read of that love, so great, so true,
    Love everlasting, yet ever new;
For who can tell but his heart may be won!

Read to him, Connie! For it may be
    That your Sunday book, like a silver bar
    Of steady light from a guiding star,

May gleam in memory, clear and far,
Across the waves of a wintry sea.

Baby's Turn.

Tiny feet so busy in a tiny patter out of sight,
Little hands escaping from protecting doily white,
One in lifted eagerness, and one that grasps the baby chair, —
All impatient! Baby darling, must not sister have a share?

Only just a moment, dearie; coming, coming! don't be vexed!
Only just a moment, darling; then we'll see whose turn is next!
Ah, she knows as well as we do! Baby's turn is come at last;
Now the little mouth may open; gently, gently, not too fast.

Baby's turn! To-day 'tis only for the fruit so nice and sweet,
But a far-away to-morrow hastens on with silent feet;
When the yesterdays of life are dearest in our dimming gaze,
Baby's vision will be filled with brightly realized to-days.

Baby's turn for fair unfolding in the sunny girlhood time,
For the blossom and the breezes, for the carol and the chime;
Baby's turn to wear the crown of womanhood upon her brow,
Heavier but nobler than the fairy gold which glitters now.

Baby's turn to care for others, and to kiss away the tear,
For the joy of ministration to the suffering or the dear,
For the happiness of giving help and comfort, love and life,
Whether walking all alone, or as a blessed and blessing wife.

Baby's turn for this and more, if God should give her length of days; —
For the calmness of experience and the retrospect of praise,
For the silver trace of sorrows glistening in the sunset ray,
For the evening stillness falling on the turmoil of the day.

What though Baby's turn may come for bitter griefs and wearing fears!
Love shall lighten every trial,—love that prays and love that hears.
See! she watches and she wonders till the reverie is o'er;
Did she think she was forgotten? Now 'tis Baby's turn once more!

For Charity.

The sun is burning, O little maiden,
Thou hast sweet water, is it for me?
I am so thirsty, so heavy-laden,
Give me cool water, for charity!
    Sparkling and gleaming,
    The crystal streaming
Seems but awaiting my only plea—
I am so thirsty, so heavy-laden,
Give me cool water, for charity!

O gentle maiden, I thirst no longer,
But sweeter waters thou hast for me:
Then pour them freely, from fountain stronger,
Sweet thoughts of kindness, for charity!
    The world is only
    A pathway lonely,
And hearts are waiting for sympathy;
Then pour them freely from fountain stronger
Sweet thoughts of kindness, for charity!

O little maiden, 'tis thine to brighten,
Like sparkling waters, life's lonely lea;
All grief to soften, all joy to heighten
With love and gladness, for charity!
    Thus onward flowing,
    All good bestowing,
A stream of blessing thy life shall be,
All grief to brighten, all joy to heighten
With love and gladness, for charity!

Severn Song.

The Severn flow is soft and fair, as slowly
    The light grows dim;
The sunset glow is soft and full, and holy
    As evening hymn.

We float along beneath the forest darkling,
Blending with song the silence of the hour:
We swiftly glide where rapids bright and sparkling
Bear us beside the ruddy rock and tower.
    O softly, softly row in measured time,
      While nearer, nearer swells the curfew chime.
Now, now again adown the current shooting,
        New joy we hail;
While through the forest thrills the fairy fluting
        Of nightingale.
O sweet and sweeter that hidden lay,
That in the twilight dies away.
Then merrily onward! O merrily row!
And smoothly swift, O Severn, flow!

The Severn flow is swift and strong, as neareth
        The home we love;
The sunset glow has paled and passed, and cleareth
        The heaven above.
The children's eyes will soon be gently closing,
Calm stars arise and shine on earth instead;
And through the night, all peacefully reposing,
Angels of light shall guard each tiny bed.
    O swiftly, swiftly row o'er darkening stream,
      While nearer, nearer shines the home lamp's gleam.
Now, now awake the song of purest thrilling,
        Of home and love;
And call the echoes forth, with music filling
        The rocks above.
Our song is sweetest as falls the day,
For we are on our homeward way:
Then merrily onward! O merrily row!
And smoothly swift, O Severn, flow!

My Mother's Request.

(SUNDAY MORNING, 8 O'CLOCK.)

THE Sabbath morn dawns o'er the mountain brow,
And lights the earth with glory soft and mild:

Oh, think'st thou, dearest mother, even now
Of me, thy youngest and most wayward child?

For this, my mother, is the sacred hour
When thou didst bid me ever think of thee:
Oh, surely nothing earthly could have power
To break the spell which hallows it to me.

Thy loving look, thy feeble voice, I seem,
Though years have passed, to see and hear again;
Not as the shadowy fancies of a dream,
But as distinct, as vivid now as then.

"When in my Saviour's glorious home I dwell,
Forget not this my last request to thee:
When soundeth forth the early Sabbath bell,
Where'er thou art, my Fanny, think of me!"

Oh, why was this thy dying wish—thy last?
Thou would'st not think that I should e'er forget
My mother's love, that passing years might cast
A cloudy veil where that bright star did set;

Thou could'st not wish to wake the grief anew
Which Time's dark poppies might have lulled awhile;
'Twas not that tear-drops might again bedew
My cheek for aye, and chase again each smile.

Oh no! were death an endless, joyless sleep,
Thou hadst not bid me on thy memory dwell;
This hour for thee thou hadst not bid me keep,
To grieve thy child, thou lovèdst her too well.

But well thou knew'st I could not think of thee
Without remembering Him with whom thou art,
To whom thou oft didst pray so fervently
That I might give my wandering, wilful heart.

I must remember too the joyful faith
Which filled thy soul e'en in thy dying hour,
And led thee calmly through the vale of death;
There I must ever see its wondrous power.

I could not but fulfil thy last desire,
The last sweet echo of thy loving voice,
Calling my mind each Sabbath morning higher,
Where thou in endless Sabbath dost rejoice.

So if my heart should tempt me to forget
To watch and pray, and Jesu's love to seek,
This quiet hour might break for me the net,
And free my feet afresh each opening week.

Oft when I wavered, slipped, and nearly fell,
Yet stunned and giddy heeded not my fate,
The fatal charm was broken by that bell,
Thy memory oped my eyes ere yet too late.

And oft when sad and hopeless seemed my way,
Its sweet sound told me of the victory
Which thy bright faith hath gained, and then a ray
Of hope hath whispered, " Such may be for thee."

Oh, 'twas a mother's love which did devise
This gentle way of helping her child's soul;
Not on earth only, but from yon bright skies
To aid her steps towards the heavenly goal.

Oh, Thou who dwellest with Thy ransomed, where
The one long Sabbath ne'er may darkly close,
By Thy rich mercy grant this earliest prayer,
Which oft for me from her dear lips arose.

Bring me, oh, bring me to Thy house of light,
That there with my loved mother I may dwell,
And e'er rejoicing in Thy presence bright,
May praise Thy love, who doest all things well.

At Home To-night.

I.

The lessons are done and the prizes won,
    And the counted weeks are past;

O the holiday joys of the girls and boys
    Who are "home to-night" at last!
O the ringing beat of the springing feet,
    As into the hall they rush!
O the tender bliss of the first home kiss,
    With its moment of fervent hush!
So much to tell and to hear as well,
    As they gather around the glow!
Who would not part, for the joy of heart
    That only the parted can know—
        At home to-night!

II.

But all have not met, there are travellers yet
    Speeding along through the dark,
By tunnel and bridge, past river and ridge,
    To the distant, yet nearing mark.
But hearts are warm, for the winter storm
    Has never a chill for love;
And faces are bright in the flickering light
    Of the small dim lamp above.
And voices of gladness rise over the madness
    Of the whirl and the rush and the roar,
For rapid and strong it bears them along
    To a home and an open door—
        Yes, home to-night!

III.

Oh, home to-night, yes, home to-night,
    Through the pearly gate and the open door!
Some happy feet on the golden street
    Are entering now to "go out no more."
For the work is done and the rest begun,
    And the training time is for ever past,
And the home of rest in the mansions blest
    Is safely, joyously reached at last.
O the love and light in that home to-night!
    O the songs of bliss and the harps of gold!

O the glory shed on the new-crowned head!
  O the telling of love that can ne'er be told—
O the welcome that waits at the shining gates,
  For those who are following far, yet near;
When all shall meet at His glorious feet
  In the light and the love of His home so dear!
    Yes, "home to-night!"

Note. —These verses, written a few days before Christmas, were suggested by the remark of a young friend, after picturing the merry "breaking up" of her old school-fellows,—"They will all be at home to-night." The thought arose—"Perhaps some of Christ's little ones, who have been learning in His school, may be reaching His home to-night!" And while the third stanza was being written, a telegram came bearing the sad and unexpected tidings that a dear little girl of twelve years old had indeed just reached home, after a short illness, and entered the presence of the Saviour whom she had early learnt to love. The coincidence of the thought with the very hour of her departure, being unconnected with any idea of her illness, was remarkable.

An Indian Flag.

The golden gates were opening
  For another welcome guest;
For a ransomed heir of glory
  Was entering into rest:

The first in far Umritsur
  Who heard the joyful sound,
The first who came to Jesus
  Within its gloomy bound.

The wonderers and the watchers
  Around his dying bed,
Saw Christ's own fearless witness
  Safe through the valley led.

And they whose faithful sowing
  Had not been all in vain,
Knew that the angels waited
  Their sheaf of ripened grain.

He spoke: "Throughout the city
  How many a flag is raised

Where loveless deities are owned,
    And powerless gods are praised!

"I give my house to Jesus,
    That it may always be
A flag for Christ, the Son of God,
    Who gave Himself for me."

And now in far Umritsur
    That flag is waving bright,
Amid the heathen darkness,
    A clear and shining light.

A house where all may gather
    The words of peace to hear,
And seek the only Saviour
    Without restraint or fear;

Where patient toil of teaching,
    And kindly deeds abound;
Where holy festivals are kept,
    And holy songs resound.

First convert of Umritsur,
    Well hast thou led the way;
Now, who will rise and follow?
    Who dares to answer, "Nay"?

O children of salvation!
    O dwellers in the light!
Have ye no "flag for Jesus,"
    Far-waving, fair, and bright?

Will ye not band together,
    And, working hand in hand,
Set up a "flag for Jesus,"
    In that wide heathen land?

In many an Indian city,
    Oh, let a standard wave,
Our gift of love and honour,
    To Him who came to save;

To Him beneath whose banner
    Of wondrous love we rest;
Our Friend, the Friend of sinners
    The Greatest and the Best.

Love for Love.

1 John 4:16.

Knowing that the God on high,
    With a tender Father's grace,
Waits to hear your faintest cry,
    Waits to show a Father's face,—
Stay and think!—oh, should not you
Love this gracious Father too?

Knowing Christ was crucified,
    Knowing that He loves you now
Just as much as when He died
    With the thorns upon His brow,—
Stay and think!—oh, should not you
Love this blessèd Saviour too?

Knowing that a Spirit strives
    With your weary, wandering heart,
Who can change the restless lives,
    Pure and perfect peace impart,—
Stay and think!—oh, should not you
Love this loving Spirit too?

The Turned Lesson.

"I thought I knew it!" she said,
    "I thought I had learnt it quite!"
But the gentle Teacher shook her head,
    With a grave yet loving light
In the eyes that fell on the upturned face,
    As she gave the book
With the mark still set in the self-same place.

"I thought I knew it!" she said;
    And a heavy tear fell down,
As she turned away with bending head,
    Yet not for reproof or frown,
Not for the lesson to learn again,
    Or the play-hour lost; —
It was something else that gave the pain.

She could not have put it in words,
    But the Teacher understood,
As God understands the chirp of the birds
    In the depth of an autumn wood.
And a quiet touch on the reddening cheek
    Was quite enough;
No need to question, no need to speak.

Then the gentle voice was heard,
    "Now I will try you again!"
And the lesson was mastered,—every word!
    Was it not worth the pain?
Was it not kinder the task to turn,
    Than to let it pass,
As a lost, lost leaf that she did not learn?

Is it not often so,
    That we only learn in part,
And the Master's testing-time may show
    That it was not quite "by heart"?
Then He gives, in His wise and patient grace,
    That lesson again
With the mark still set in the self-same place.

Only, stay by His side
    Till the page is really known,
It may be we failed because we tried
    To learn it all alone.
And now that He would not let us lose
    One lesson of love
(For He knows the loss)—can we refuse?

But oh! how *could* we dream
    That we knew it all so well?
Reading so fluently, as we deem,
    What we could not even spell!
And oh! how could we grieve once more
    That patient One
Who has turned so many a task before?

That waiting One, who now
    Is letting us try again;
Watching us with the patient brow
    That bore the wreath of pain;
Thoroughly teaching what He would teach,
    Line upon line,
Thoroughly doing His work in each.

Then let our hearts "be still,"
    Though our task is turned to-day.
Oh let Him teach us what He will,
    In His own gracious way,
Till, sitting only at Jesu's feet,
    As we learn each line,
The hardest is found all clear and sweet!

My Singing Lesson.

ABSTRACT.

HERE beginneth—chapter the first of a series,
To be followed by manifold notes and queries;
So novel the queries, so trying the notes,
I think I must have the queerest of throats,
And most notable dullness, or else long ago
The Signor had given up teaching, I trow.
I wonder if ever before he has taught
A pupil who can't do a thing as she ought!

The voice has machinery—(now to be serious),
Invisible, delicate, strange, and mysterious.

A wonderful organ-pipe firstly we trace,
Which is small in a tenor and wide in a bass;
Below an Æolian harp is provided,
Through whose fairy-like fibres the air will be guided.
Above is an orifice, larger or small
As the singer desires to rise or to fall;
Expand and depress it to deepen your roar,
But raise and contract it when high you would soar.
Alas for the player, the pipes, and the keys,
If the bellows give out an inadequate breeze!
So this is the method of getting up steam,
The one motive power for song or for scream:
Slowly and deeply, and just like a sigh,
Fill the whole chest with a mighty supply;
Through the mouth only, and not through the nose,
And the lungs must condense it ere farther it goes
(*How* to condense it, I really don't know,
And very much hope the next lesson will show).
Then, forced from each side, through the larynx it comes,
And reaches the region of molars and gums,
And half of the sound will be ruined or lost
If by any impediment here it is crossed.
On the soft of the palate beware lest it strike,
The effect would be such as your ear would not like.
And arch not the tongue, or the terrified note
Will straightway be driven back into the throat.
Look well to your trigger, nor hasten to pull it:
Once hear the report and you've done with your bullet.
In the feminine voice there are registers three,
Which upper, and middle, and lower must be;
And each has a sounding-board all of its own,
The chest, lips, and head, to reverberate tone.
But in cavities nasal it never must ring,
Or no one is likely to wish you to sing.
And if on this subject you waver in doubt,
By listening and feeling the truth will come out.
The lips, by the bye, will have plenty to do
In forming the vowels Italian and true;

Eschewing the English, uncertain and hideous,
With an *O* and a *U* that are simply amphibious,
In flexible freedom let both work together,
And the under one must not be stiffened like leather.

Here endeth the substance of what I remember,
Indited this twenty-sixth day of November.

Leaning over the Waterfall.

A young lady, aged 20, fell over the rocks at the Swallow Waterfall in the summer of 1873, and was lost to sight in a moment. The body was not recovered till four hours afterwards.

   LEANING over the waterfall!
    Lured by the fairy sight,
   Heeding not the warning call,
    Watching the foam and the flow,
   Smooth and dark, or swift and bright,
   Here in the shade and there in the light!
     Oh, who could know
   The coming sorrow, the nearing woe!

Leaning over the waterfall!
  Only a day before
She had spoken of Jesu's wondrous call,
  As He trod the waves of Galilee.
They asked, as she gazed from the sunset shore,
"If He walked that water, what would you do?"
Then fell the answer, glad and true,
  "If He beckoned me,
I would go to Him on the pathless sea."

Leaning over the waterfall
  Only a moment before!
And then the slip, the helpless call,
  The plunge unheard in the pauseless roar
  By the startled watchers on the shore;
And the feet that stood by the waterfall,
  So fair and free,
Are standing with Christ by the crystal sea.

Leaning over the waterfall!
    Have you not often leant
(What should hinder? or what appall?)
Freely, fearlessly, over the brink,
    Merrily glancing adown the stream,
    Or gazing wrapt in a musical dream
At the lovely waters? But pause and think —
    Who kept *your* feet,
And suffered you not such death to meet?

Leaning over the waterfall!
    What if *your* feet had slipped?
Never a moment of power to call,
    Never a hand in time to save
    From the terrible rush of the ruthless wave!
Hearken! would it be ill or well
    If thus *you* fell?
Hearken! would it be heaven or hell?

Leaning over the waterfall!
    Listen, and learn, and lean!
Listen to Him whose loving call
    Soundeth deep in your heart to-day!
    Learn of Jesus, the only way,
How to be holy, how to be blest!
    Lean on His breast,
And yours shall be safety and joy and rest.

"*That's not the Way at Sea.*"

Reply of Captain Bourchier of the training-ship *Goliath,* when his boys entreated him to save himself from the burning wreck. 1876.

HE stood upon the fiery deck,
    Our Captain kind and brave!
He would not leave the burning wreck,
    While there was one to save.
We wanted him to go before,
    And we would follow fast;

We could not bear to leave him there,
    Beside the blazing mast.
But his voice rang out in a cheery shout,
    And noble words spoke he, —
"That's not the way at sea, my boys,
    That's not the way at sea!"

So each one did as he was bid,
    And into the boats we passed,
While closer came the scorching flame,
    And our Captain was the last.
Yet once again he dared his life,
    One little lad to save;
Then we pulled to shore from the blaze and roar,
    With our Captain kind and brave.
In the face of Death, with its fiery breath,
    He had stood,—and so would we!
For that's the way at sea, my boys,
    For that's the way at sea!

Now let the noble words resound,
    And echo far and free,
Wherever English hearts are found,
    On English shore or sea.
The iron nerve of duty, joined
    With golden vein of love,
Can dare to do, and dare to wait,
    With courage from above.
Our Captain's shout among the flames
    A watchword long shall be,—
"That's not the way at sea, my boys,
    That's not the way at sea!"

The Awakening.

So it has come to you, dear,
    Come so soon!
Come in the sunshine early,
Come in the morning pearly,
    Not in the blaze of noon.

Yes, it has come to you, dear,
    Strange and sweet;
Come ere the merry May-time
Melts to the glowing hay-time,
   Hushed in the sultry heat.

Come—with mysterious shadow,
    Weird and new,—
Come with a magic lustre
Hung on the shining cluster
   Ripening fast for you.

Come! and the exquisite minor,
    Rich and deep,
Swells with Æolian blending
Chords of the spirit, ending
   Boyhood's enchanted sleep.

Sleep that is past for ever!
    Is it gain?
What does the waking seem like?
Love that is only dream-like
   Sings not a truthful strain.

Hearts that have roused and listened
    Never more,
(Though they may miss the crossed tones,
Though they may mourn the lost tones,)
   Sleep as they slept before.

Come! and the great transition
    Now is past!
Never again the boy-life,
Only the pain—and joy-life,
   More of the first than last.

Come! and they do not guess it,
    Why such a change!
Why should the mirth and riot
Tone into manly quiet!
   Is it not passing strange?

Come! 'Tis a night of wonder
    At this call.
Characters cabalistic,
Writings all dim and mystic
    Tremble upon the wall.

Come! am I glad or sorry?
    Wait and see!
Wait for God's silent moulding,
Wait for His full unfolding,
    Wait for the days to be.

Something to Do.

"SOMETHING to do, mamma, something to do!"
    Who has not heard the cry?
    Something to plan and something to try!
Something to do when the sky is blue,
    And the sun is clear and high;
Something to do on a rainy day,
Tired of lessons or tired of play;
Something to do in the morning walk,
Better than merely to stroll and talk.
For the fidgety feet, oh, something to do,
For the mischievous fingers something too;
For the busy thought in the little brain,
    For the longing love of the little heart,
Something easy, and nice, and plain;
    Something in which they can all take part;
Something better than breakable toys,
Something for girls and something for boys!
I know, I know, and I'll tell you too,
Something for all of you now to do!

First, you must listen! Do you know
Where the poor sick children go?
Think of hundreds all together
In the pleasant summer weather,

Lying sadly day by day,
Having pain instead of play;
No dear mother sitting near,
    No papa to kiss good-night;
Brothers, sisters, playmates dear,
    All away and out of sight.
Little feet that cannot go
Where the pink-tipped daisies grow;
Little eyes that never see
Bud or blossom, bird or tree;
Little hands that folded lie
As the weary weeks go by.
What if you could send them flowers,
Brightening up the dismal hours?

Then the hospitals for others,
For the fathers and the mothers;
Where the weary sufferers lie,
    While the weeks go slowly past,
    Some with hope of cure at last,
Some to suffer till they die.
Now, while you are scampering free,
In your happy spring-tide glee,
They are lying sadly there,
Weak and sick—oh, don't you care?
Don't you want to cheer each one?
Don't you wish it could be done?

Then the poor old people too,
    In the dreary workhouse-room,
Nothing all day long to do,
    Nothing to light up the gloom!
Older, weaker, every day,
All their children gone away;
Nothing pleasant, nothing bright,
For the dimming, aching sight.
Would it not be nice to send
Nosegays by some loving friend?

Then if you could only see
    Where so many thousands live,

All in sin and misery,
Dirt and noise and poverty,
   What, oh, what would you not give,
Just some little thing to do
   That might do a little good!
Don't you want to help them too?
   I will tell you how you could!
Gather flowers for Jesus' sake,
For a loving hand to take
Into all those dreadful places,
Bringing smiles to haggard faces,
Bringing tears to hardened eyes;
Bringing back the memories
Of the home so long ago
Left for wickedness and woe,
Of the time, so far away,
When they learned to sing and pray.
Oh, you cannot guess the power
Of a little simple flower!

———

And yet the message they should bear,
Of God our Father's love and care,
Is never really read aright
Without the Holy Spirit's light; —
Without the voice of Jesus, heard
In His own sweet and mighty word.
And so we *never* send the flowers
With only messages of ours;
But every group of buds and bells
The story of salvation tells.
Let every little nosegay bring
Not only fragrance of the spring,
But sweeter fragrance of His Name,
   Who saves and pardons, soothes and heals,
The living Saviour, still the Same,
   Who every pain and sorrow feels.
The little texts are sweeter far
Than lily-bell or primrose star;

And He will help you just to choose
The very words that He will use.
    To find them out and make a list
Of promise-words, so strong and bright,
So full of comfort and of light,
    That all their meaning *can't* be missed!
Think how every one may be
    God's own message from above
To some little girl or boy,
Changing sadness into joy,
Soothing some one's dreadful pain,
Making some one glad again,
    With His comfort and His love!
Calling them to Jesus' feet,
Showing them what He has done!
Darlings, will it not be sweet
    If He blesses only one?
Only *one?* Nay, ask Him still,
    Ask Him *every one* to bless!
He can do it, and He will;
Do not let us ask Him less!

Now then, set to work at once,
If you're not a thorough dunce!
Cut the little holders squarely,
    Keep the edges smooth and straight:
Now the paint-box: artists bold!
    Paint the borders firm and fairly
With your prettiest red or gold!
    Easy this, at any rate.
Now for writing—clearest, neatest,
    (Or it may be gently hinted,
    Better still if neatly printed.)
Tracing words the strongest, sweetest,—
Words that must and will avail,
Though the loveliest blossoms fail.
Then away, away, the first fine day!
Follow the breeze that is out at play,

Something to Do.

Follow the bird and follow the bee,
Follow the butterfly flitting free,
   For I think they know
Where the sweetest wildflowers grow;
Bluebells in the shady dingle,
Where the violet-odours mingle;
Where the fairy primrose lamp
   Seems to light the hawthorn shade;
Orchis in the meadow damp,
   Cowslip in the sunny glade.
(But not the pale anemone,
For that will fade so speedily.)
Hedge and coppice, lane and field,
Gather all the store they yield!
Buttercups and daisies too,
Though so little prized by you,
Will be gold and silver treasure,
In their power of giving pleasure
To the poor in city alleys,
Far away from hills and valleys,
Who have never seen them grow
Since their childhood, long ago;
Or to children pale and small,
Who never saw them grow at all!
And don't forget the fair green leaves
   That have their own sweet tales to tell,
And waving grass that humbly weaves
   The emerald robe of bank and dell.
Is there some one at home who cannot go
To gather the flowers as they grow?
Then there is plenty for her to do
In making the nosegays up for you;
Getting them ready to travel away,
In time for the work of the coming day.

But oh, how busy you will be
   When the packing must be done!
Oh, the bustle and the glee,
   Will it not be famous fun?

And when the box is gone away,
    The pleasure need not all be past
    I think it will not be the last!
Just set to work another day!
    And send some more
    From the beautiful store
Which God keeps sending you fresh and new,
    And thank Him too
That He has given you "SOMETHING TO DO!"

Little Nora.

FAR off upon a western shore,
    Where wildest billows roam,
Beneath the great grim rocks there stands
    A tiny cabin home;

And in it dwells a little one,
    With eyes of laughing blue,
And lips as red as any rose
    With early sparkling dew.

Her father was a fisher, and
    Went out with every tide,
While Nora sat and watched alone
    By her sick mother's side.

It was a weary thing to sit
    For many a long, long day,
Without a ramble on the beach,
    Or e'en a thought of play;

But Nora did not think it hard,
    She loved her mother so,
And in a thousand ways she tried
    Her earnest love to show.

One day she left the cabin door,
    And walked a long, long way—
Now high upon the breezy cliffs,
    Now close to ocean spray.

She went to seek some remedy
    To ease her mother's pain,
Tho' little hope there was that she
    Could e'er be well again.

The ruby clouds have curtained o'er
    The golden glowing west,
Where 'neath the white-winged wavelets now
    The sun hath gone to rest;

But little Nora comes not yet!
    The mother's fears arise,
The evening breeze brings nothing save
    The seabird's mournful cries.

The twilight hour is passing fast
    In weariness and pain,
She waits and listens for her child,
    As yet she waits in vain.

Hark, hark! a bounding step is heard
    Along the pebbly shore,
And now a tiny hand is laid
    Upon the cabin door;

"Oh, mother, darling mother, I
    Have such good news to tell!
Far more than medicine I have brought
    To make you glad and well!"

More brightly gleamed her joyous eye,
    And rosier grew her cheek,
While forth she poured the happy words,
    As fast as tongue could speak.

"I bought the medicine, mother dear,
    And turned to come away,
When by me stood a kind grave man,
    And gently bade me stay;

"And then he spoke sweet words to me,
    About the Saviour's love,

And of the glorious home where all
    His children meet above.

"He told me Jesus loved us so
    That He came down to die,
And suffered all instead of us;—
    And then it made me cry:

"He said His blood was quite enough
    To wash our sins away,
And make us fit for Heaven at once
    If we should die to-day.

"So, mother dear, we shall not need
    To purgatory go;
If Jesus has forgiven all,
    That is enough, you know!"

The rosy glow had rested on
    The mother's whitening cheek;
'Twas fading now, and Nora ceased—
    Then came a long wild shriek,—

"Oh, mother, speak to me once more, —
    Oh, is she really dead?"
'Twas even so, the hand was cold,
    And stilled the throbbing head;

Yes, even while those blessèd words
    Like angel-music fell,
Her weary spirit passed away,
    But whither! who may tell?

Oh, bitter were the tears which fell
    From little Nora's eye,
And many a day and night had passed
    Ere they again were dry.

But bitterest were they when she thought,
    "Oh, I can never tell
If with that blessèd Saviour now,
    Sweet mother, thou dost dwell!

"Ah! had I only sooner known
    What I have heard to-day,
I would have told her more of Him
    Before she went away;

"For perhaps she did not hear me then,
    So she could never know
The way that Jesus Christ has made
    To His bright home to go.

"I love Him, yes, I'm sure I do,
    Then He will take me home
To be with Him for evermore,
    Where sorrow cannot come;

"But oh, I cannot bear to think,
    When I His glory see,
And rest within the Saviour's arms—
    Where will my mother be?"

Dear children, you have learnt the way
    To that bright home above,
You have been told of Jesus and
    His deep and tender love;

In Ireland there are little ones
    Whose hearts are very sad,
Oh, won't you try and send to them
    Sweet words to make them glad?

"Come over and Help Us."

The Irish child's cry.

OH, children of England, beyond the blue sea,
Your poor little brothers and sisters are we;
'Tis not much affection or pity we find,
But we hear you are loving and gentle and kind;
So will you not listen a minute or two,
While we tell you a tale that is all of it true?

We live in a cabin, dark, smoky, and poor;
At night we lie down on the hard dirty floor;
Our clothes are oft tattered, and shoes we have none;
Our food we must beg, as we always have done;
So cold and so hungry, and wretched are we,
It would make you quite sad if you only could see.

There's no one to teach us poor children to read;
There's no one to help us, and no one to lead;
There's no one at all that will tell us the way
To be happy or safe, or teach us to pray:
To the bright place above us we all want to go,
But we cannot,—for how to get there we don't know.

They tell us the Virgin will hear if we call,
But sure in one minute she can't hear us all.
And the saints are too busy in Heaven, we hear;
Then often the priests make us tremble with fear
At the fire of purgatory, which, as they tell,
Is almost as dreadful as going to hell.

Oh, will you not help us, and send us a ray
Of the light of the Gospel, to brighten our way?
Oh, will you not tell us the beautiful story
Of Jesus, who came from His dwelling of glory
To save little children, and not only you,
But even the poor ragged Irish ones too?

The English Child's Reply.

We have heard the call from your fair green Isle;
    Our hearts have wept at your saddening tale;
And we long to waken a brighter smile
    By a story of love which shall never fail.

We should like you to come to our Bible-land,
    And share our comforts and blessings too;
We would take you all with a sister's hand,
    And try to teach and to gladden you.

But you're so far off that it cannot be,
    And we have no wings, or to you we'd fly;
So we'll try to send o'er the foaming sea
    Sweet words to brighten each heavy eye,—

Sweet words of Him, who was once so poor,
    That He had not where to lay His head;
But hath opened now the gleaming door
    To the palace of light, where His feast is spread.

There you may enter; He calls each one,—
    You're as welcome there as the greatest king!
Come to Him then, for He casts out none,
    And nothing at all do you need to bring.

He will change your rags for a robe of white,
    An angel-harp, and a crown of gold;
You may dwell for aye in His presence bright,
    And the beaming smiles of His love behold.

We will gladly save from our little store
    Our pennies, our farthings, from day to day,
And only wish we could do far more;
    But for Erin's children we'll always pray.

A Plea for the Little Ones.

It was Easter Monday morning,
    A dull and showery day;
We were sorry for the children
    Who could not run and play.

I heard the sound of singing
    As I passed along the street—
An unseen tiny chorus
    Of tiny voices sweet.

Beneath a sheltering doorway,
    Safe from the April weather
Eight happy little singers
    Sat lovingly together,

Five crowding on the doorstep
    With arms entwined, and three
On broken stool or baby chair,
    Close clustering knee to knee.

They sang about the "happy land,"
    So very "far away,"
And happier faces never shone
    In any game of play.

And then they sang it all again,
    And gently rocked each other;
Then said the little leader,
    "Now let us sing another!"

"Now *I* will say a hymn to you!"
    (Oh, the sixteen eyes were bright!)
So I said them "Little Jessie,"
    As they listened with delight.

JESSIE'S FRIEND.

"Little Jessie, darling pet,
    Do you want a Friend?
One who never will forget,
    Loving to the end?
One whom you can tell, when sad
    Everything that grieves,
One who loves to make you glad,
    One who never leaves?

"Such a loving Friend is ours,
    Near us all the day,
Helping us in lesson-hours,
    Smiling on our play;
Keeping us from doing wrong,
    Guarding everywhere;
Listening to each happy song,
    And each little prayer.

"Jessie, if you only knew
    What He is to me,
Surely you would love Him too,
    You would 'come and see.'
Come, and you will find it true,
    Happy you will be!
Jesus says, and says to you,
    'Come, oh come, to Me.'"

"Now tell me who, if you can guess,
    Was little Jessie's Friend?
Who is the Friend that loves so much,
    And loveth to the end?"

I would that you had seen the smile
    On every sunny face;
It made a palace of delight
    Out of that dismal place,

As, reverently yet joyously,
    They answered without fear,
"It's Jesus!" That belovèd Name
    Had never seemed more dear.

And then we talked awhile of Him—
    They knew the story well;
His holy life, His precious death,
    Those rosy lips could tell.

All beautiful, and wonderful,
    And sweet and true it seemed,
Such hold no fairy tale had gained
    That ever fancy dreamed.

So, to be good and kind all day
    These little children tried,
Because they knew *He* was so good,
    Because *He* bled and died.

Blest knowledge! Oh, what human lore
    Can be compared with such!
"Who taught you this, dear little ones?
    Where did you learn so much?"

Again the bright eyes cheerily
    Looked up from step and stool;
They answered (mark the answer well!),
    "*We learnt it all at school!*"

At school, at school! And shall we take
    The Book of books away!
Withhold it from the little ones?
    Leave them at will to stray—

Upon dark mountains, helplessly,
    Without the guiding light
That God entrusts to *us,* until
    They perish in the night?

What was the world before that Book
    Went forth in glorious night?
Availed the lore of Greece and Rome
    To chase its Stygian night?

We send the messengers of life
    To many a distant strand.
And shall we tie the tongues that teach
    The poor of our own land?

Shall husks and chaff, be freely given,
    And not the Bread of Life?
And shall the Word of Peace become
    A centre of mad strife?

Shall those who name the Name of Christ
    His own great gift withhold?
Our Lamp, our Chart, our Sword, our Song,
    Our Pearl, our most fine Gold!

Why would ye have "no Bible taught"?
    Is it for *fear?* or shame?

Out, out upon such coward hearts,
    False to their Master's name!

If God be God, if truth be truth,
    If Christian men be men,
Let them arise and fight the fight,
    Though it were one to ten!

With battle-cry of valiant faith,
    Let Britain's sons arise,—
"Our children *shall* be taught the Word
    That only maketh wise!"

So, dauntlessly, will we unfurl
    Our banner bright and broad,
The cause of His dear Word of Life,
    Our cause, the Cause of God.

Two Rings.

SHE stood by the western window,
    In the midsummer twilight fair;
And the sunset breeze leaped from the trees
    To lift her heavy hair.

Loving and lingering that good-night,
    Which again and again was said,
As ever a fresh excuse was found
    To "put off going to bed."

She took a ring from the table,
    Blue, with a diamond eye;
A forget-me-not that would never fade
    'Neath any wintry sky.

She placed it on her little hand,
    And danced with sudden glee;
"Look at my ring, my pretty ring!
    It is mine just now, you see!"

She laughed her merry ringing laugh,
    I answered with a sigh,
Strange echo to my darling's mirth,
    Though scarcely knowing why.

Her childish beauty touched my heart,
    And rose to a vision fair
Of far-off days, when another ring
    That little hand might wear.

And mine—it might be pulseless then
    Under the churchyard tree;
So I drew her gently to my side,
    And took her on my knee.

"It shall be yours, my darling,"
    I said; "but not to-day;
It *shall* be yours, my darling,
    When I am gone away."

She glanced up quickly in my face,
    Not sure that she heard aright;
And the shadow that fell in the sweet brown eyes
    Was sweeter than any light.

Then she bent her head and kissed the ring,
    With a kiss both grave and long;
Hardly the kiss of a little child,
    So fervent and so strong.

And hardly the tones of a little child,
    That spoke so earnestly,—
"Yes; I will always wear it,
    Mine it shall always be.

"But oh!" (and the eyes, love-brightened,
    Shone with a sudden tear),
"I hope I shall never wear it,
    Never, oh never, dear!"

Five summers smoothly passed away,
    And the sixth was drawing nigh,
While herald glory woke the earth,
    And filled the dazzling sky.

An April morning, radiant
    With June-like gleam and glow,
Arose as fair as if the world
    No shade of grief could know.

A tiny packet came for me,
    With many a dark-edged fold,
And safe within it lay a ring,—
    A little ring of gold.

Oh, well I knew its carving quaint
    Of old ancestral days;
Last seen upon a waving hand
    In slanting autumn rays.

O fair young hand, that waved good-bye
    With passing grace and glee!
We knew not that it was farewell,—
    The *last* farewell for me.

The sweet bright spring that touched the earth
    With all-renewing might,
For *her* eternal beauty brought,
    Eternal life and light.

All through the solemn Passion week
    She lay so still and sweet,
A carven lily, white and pure,
    For God's own temple meet;—

Until the day when Jesus died,
    The Saviour whom she knew,
The Shepherd whom she followed home
    The shadowy portal through.

And when the evening gently closed
    That sad and sacred day,

They left the last kiss on her brows,
 And took the ring away.

———

Two rings are always on my hand,
 The azure and the gold,
And they shall gleam together till
 My tale of life is told.

A Mountain Cantata.

"That Thy name is near, Thy wondrous works declare."—Psalm 75:1.

The Mountain Maidens.

(Zella, Dora, Lisetta.)

A CANTATA.

Part I.—Sunrise.

(1.) Dawn Chorus.

The stars die out, and the moon grows dim,
    Slowly, softly, the dark is paling!
Comes o'er the eastern horizon-rim,
    Slowly, softly, a bright unveiling.

The white mist floats in the vale at rest,
    Ghostly, dimly, a silver shiver;
The golden east and the purple west
    Flushing deep with a crimson quiver.

The mountains gleam with expectant light,
    Near and grandly, or far and faintly,
In festal robing of solemn white,
    Waiting, waiting, serene and saintly.

Lo! on the mountain-crest, sudden and fair,
Bright herald of morning, the rose-tint is there;
Peak after peak lighteth up with the glow
That crowneth with ruby the Alpine snow.

Summit on summit, and crest beyond crest,
The beacons are spreading away to the west;
Crimson and fire, and amber and rose,
Touch with life and with glory the Alpine snows.

(2.) Chorale.

Father, who hast made the mountains,
    Who hast formed each tiny flower,
Who hast filled the crystal fountains,
    Who hast sent us sun and shower:
Hear Thy children's morning prayer,
Asking for Thy guardian care;
Keep and guide us all the day,
Lead us safely all the way.

Let Thy glorious creation
    Be the whisper of Thy power;
New and wondrous revelation
    Still unfolding every hour.
Let the blessing of Thy love
Rest upon us from above;
And may evening gladness be
Full of thanks and praise to Thee.

(3.) Recitative.—*Dora.*

Our pleasant summer work begins. You go,
O merry Zella, with the obedient herd
To upland pastures, singing all the way.
And you, Lisetta, to the sterner heights,
Where only foot of Alpine goat may pass,
Or step of mountain maiden. It is mine
To work at home preparing smooth white cheese
For winter store, and often needed gain.
And mine the joy of welcoming once more
My loving sisters when the evening falls.

(4.) Song.—*Dora*.

The morning light flingeth
    Its wakening ray,
And as the day bringeth
    The work of the day,
The happy heart singeth;
    Awake and away!

No life can be dreary
    When work is delight;
Though evening be weary,
    Rest cometh at night;
And all will be cheery,
    If faithful and right.

When duty is treasure,
    And labour a joy,
How sweet is the leisure
    Of ended employ!
Then only can pleasure
    Be free from alloy.

[Repeat v. 1.]

(5.) Song.—*Zella*.

Away, away! with the break of day,
    To the sunny upland slope!
Away, away! while the earliest ray
    Tells of radiant joy and hope.

With the gentle herd that know the word
    Of kindness and of care,
While with footsteps free they follow me,
    As I lead them anywhere.

Away, away! with a merry lay,
    And the chime of a hundred bells;
Away, away! with a carol gay,
    And an echo from the fells.

  To the pastures high, where the shining sky
    Looks down on a wealth of flowers;
  To the sapphire spots, where forget-me-nots
    Smile on through lonely hours.

Away, away! while the breezes play
  In the fragrant summer morn;
Away, away! while the rock-walls grey
  Resound with the Alpen-horn.

  To the crags, all bright in the golden light
    With floral diadems,
  As fresh and fair, as "rich and rare,"
    As any royal gems.

Away, away! while the rainbow spray
  Wreaths the silver waterfalls;
Away, away! Oh, I cannot stay
  When the voice of the morning calls!

    (6.) RECITATIVE.—*Lisetta.*

Adieu, my Dora! Zella dear, adieu!
The quick light tinkle of the goat-bells now
Reminds me they are waiting for my call,
To follow where small flowers have dared to peep
And laugh, beside the glacier and the snow.
I shall not go alone, your love shall go with me.

    (7.) DUET.—*Zella and Dora.*

  Adieu, adieu till eventide!
    The hours will quickly pass,
  The shadow of the rocks will glide
    Across the sunny grass.
  We shall not mourn the lessening light,
  For we shall meet at home to-night.

  Adieu, adieu till eventide!
    The hour of home and rest,

The hour that finds us side by side,
    The sweetest and the best.
For love is joy, and love is light,
    And we shall meet at home to-night!

Adieu, adieu till eventide!
    'Tis but a little while!
We would not stay the morning's pride,
    Or noontide's dazzling smile.
But welcome evening's waning light,
For we shall meet at home to-night!

Part II.—Noon.

(8.) Song.—*Lisetta.*

It is noon upon the mountains, and the breeze has died away,
And the rainbow of the morning passes from the torrent spray,
And a calm of golden silence falls upon the glistening snow,
While the shadows of the noon-clouds rest upon the glen below.

It is noon upon the mountains, noon upon the giant rocks;
Hushed the tinkle of the goat-bells, and the bleating of the flocks;
They are sleeping on the gentians, and upon the craggy height,
In the glow of Alpine noon-tide, in the glory of the light.

It is noon upon the mountains: I will rest beside the snow,
Glittering summits far above me, blue-veined glaciers far below;
I will rest upon the gentians, till the quiet shadows creep,
Cool and soft, along the mountains, waking me from pleasant sleep.

(9.) Noon Chorus.

Rest! while the noon is high,
    Rest while the glow
Falls from the summer sky
    Over the snow.

Rest! where the Alpen-rose
    Crimsons the height,
Piercing the mountain-snows,
    Purpling the light.

Rest! while the waterfalls,
    Murmuring deep
Far-away lullabies,
    Hush thee to sleep.
        Rest! while the noon, etc.

Rest! where the mountains rise,
    Shining and white;
Piercing the deep blue skies,
    Solemn and bright.
Sleep! while the silence falls,
    Soothing to rest,
Sweetest of lullabies,
    Calming and blest.
        Rest! while the noon, etc.

(10.) RECITATIVE.—*Lisetta.*

Where am I? I was sleeping by the snow
Upon the Alpen-roses in the noon.
But am I dreaming now? The sun is low,
'Tis twilight in the valley, and I hear
No music of the goat-bells. Oh, I fear
It is no dream, but night is coming soon,
And I am all alone upon the height,
And there are small faint tracks, too quickly lost,
That need sure foot and eye in fullest light,
And crags to leap, and torrents to be crossed!
I go! may Power and Love still guard and guide aright.

(11.) SONG.—*Lisetta.*

Alone, alone! yet around me stand
    God's mountains, still and grand!
        Still and grand, serene and bright,
        Sentinels clothed in armour white,
        And helmeted with scarlet light.
            His Power is near,
            I need not fear.

Beneath the shadow of His Throne
Alone, alone, yet not alone!

Alone, alone! yet beneath me sleep
  The flowers His hand doth keep.
    Small and fair, by crag or dell,
    Trustfully closing star and bell,
    Eve by eve as twilight fell.
      His Love is near,
      I need not fear.
Beneath the rainbow of His Throne,
Alone, alone, yet not alone!

Alone, alone! yet I will not fear,
  For Power and Love are near!
    Step by step, by rock and rill,
    Trustfully onward, onward still,
    I follow home with hope and will!
      So near, so near,
      I do not fear!
Beneath the Presence of His Throne,
Alone, alone, yet not alone!

Part III.—Sunset.

(12.) S<small>UNSET</small> C<small>HORUS</small>.

It is coming, it is coming,
That marvellous up-summing,
Of the loveliest and grandest all in one:
  The great transfiguration,
  And the royal coronation,
Of the Monarch of the mountains by the priestly Sun.

  Watch breathlessly and hearken,
  While the forest throne-steps darken
His investiture in crimson and in fire;
  Not a herald-trumpet ringeth,
  Not a pæan echo flingeth,
There is music of a silence that is mightier far, and higher.

Then in radiant obedience,
A flush of bright allegiance
Lights up the vassal-summits and the proud peaks all around;
And a thrill of mystic glory
Quivers on the glaciers hoary,
As the ecstasy is full, and the mighty brow is crowned.

Crowned with ruby of resplendence
In unspeakable transcendence,
'Neath a canopy of purple and of gold outspread,
With rock-sceptres upward pointing,
While the glorious anointing
Of the consecrating sunlight is poured upon his head.

Then a swift and still transition
Falls upon the gorgeous vision,
And the ruby and the fire pass noiselessly away;
But the paling of the splendour
Leaves a rose-light, clear and tender,
And lovelier than the loveliest dream that melts before the day.

Oh to keep it, oh to hold it,
While the tremulous rays enfold it!
Oh to drink in all the beauty, and never thirst again!
Yet less lovely if less fleeting!
For the mingling and the meeting
Of the wonder and the rapture can but overflow in pain.

It is passing, it is passing!
While the softening glow is glassing
In the crystal of the heavens all the fairest of its rose.
Ever faintly and more faintly,
Ever saintly and more saintly,
Gleam the snowy heights around us in holiest repose.

O pure and perfect whiteness!
O mystery of brightness
Upon those still, majestic brows shed solemnly abroad!
Like the calm and blessèd sleeping
Of saints in Christ's own keeping,
When the smile of holy peace is left, last witness for their God.

(13.) Song.—*Dora.*

The tuneful chime of the herd is still,
    For the milking hour is past,
And tinkle, tinkle, along the hill,
    The goat-bells come at last.
But sister, sister, where art thou?
We watch and wait for thy coming now.

The crimson fades from the farthest height,
    And the rose-fire pales away;
And softly, softly, the shroud of night
    Enfolds the dying day.
But sister, sister, where art thou?
We watch and wait for thy coming now.

The cold wind swells from the icy steep,
    And the pine-trees quake and moan;
And darkly, darkly the grey clouds creep,
    And thou art all alone.
O sister, sister, where art thou?
We watch and wait for thy coming now.

(14.) Duet.—*Zella and Dora.*

We will seek thee, we will find thee,
    Though the night-winds howl and sweep!
We will follow through the torrent,
    We will follow up the steep.
Follow where the Alpen-roses
    Make the mountain all aglow,
Follow, follow through the forest,
    Follow, follow to the snow!
And our Alpine call shall echo
    From the rock and from the height,
Till a gladder tone rebounding,
Thine own merry voice resounding,
    Fill us with a great delight.

Lisetta! Lisetta!
Hush and hearken! Call again!
Lisetta! Lisetta!
Hearken, hearken! All in vain!

We will seek thee, we will find thee,
    In the wary chamois' haunt;
Toil and terror, doubt and danger,
    Loving hearts shall never daunt!
We will follow in the darkness,
    We will follow in the light;
Follow, follow till we find thee,
    Through the noon or through the night.
We will seek thee, we will find thee,
    Never weary till we hear,
Over all the torrents' rushing,
Joyous answer clearly gushing,
    Thine own Alpine echo dear!
Lisetta! Lisetta!
Hush and hearken! All in vain!
Lisetta! Lisetta!
Hearken, hearken! Call again!

(15.) TRIO.—*Zella, Dora, and Lisetta.*

LISETTA *(pp)*. I am coming!
ZELLA and DORA *(f)*. She is coming!
LISETTA *(p)*. I am coming, wait for me!
ZELLA and DORA *(p)*. She is coming!
LISETTA *(mf)*. I am coming!
ZELLA and DORA *(f)*. Come, oh come, we wait for thee!
    Nearer, nearer comes the echo,
        Nearer, nearer comes the voice,
    Nearer, nearer fall the footsteps,
        Making us indeed rejoice.
LISETTA. I am coming, wait for me!
ZELLA and DORA. Come, oh come, we wait for thee!

The Mountain Maidens.

Zella, Dora, and Lisetta.

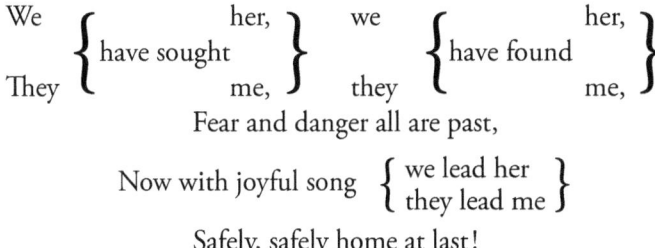

Fear and danger all are past,

Now with joyful song { we lead her / they lead me }

Safely, safely home at last!

(16.) Chorus—*Finale.*

Safe home, safe home!
Fear and danger all are past,
We are safely home at last!

Oh, the love-light shed around,
    In a rich and radiant flow,
When the lost and loved are found,
    Is the sweetest heart can know.
Fairer than the dawn-light tender,
    Fuller than the noon-tide glow,
Brighter than the sunset-splendour
    Purer than the moonlit snow.

Now let the wild cloud sweep,
    Let the wild rain pour!
Now let the avalanche leap
    With its long grand roar!
Now let the black night fall
    On the mountain crest!
Safe are our dear ones all
    In our mountain nest.

Safe home, safe home!
Fear and danger all are past,
We are safely home at last!

Arithmetical Enigma.

5/12 of the square of 3/5 of a score,
1/8 of a dozen, and 1/2 of one more,
2/5 of 1/4 of 5/9 of eighteen;
Of 25, 20, & 12 take the mean;
4/15 of 5/6 of 9/10 of one-third
Of 120, will give you a word
Which in literal truth I will
 fearlessly state
Must form the foundation of
 everything great.

——————

N.B. The initials of the above
numbers form the answer.

This "Arithmetical Enigma" was found on page 20 of F.R.H.'s Manuscript Book Nº IV, copied out in F.R.H.'s own handwriting. Please see another manuscript of this same "Arithmetical Enigma" in F.R.H.'s handwrting, an explanation, and the solution, on pages 113–114 of this book.

Enigmas and Charades.

Enigma No. 1.

An army of Cyclops, fair reader, are we,
Yet your servants especially ought we to be;
The outposts of England, 'mid ocean's roar,
We have stood since the deluge, and perhaps before.

From Parry, and Cook, and Columbus too,
A vote of thanks to ourselves is due;
But to Solomon's ships, when to Ophir sent,
Our aid, not asked, was of course not lent.

To Matilda of Flanders' assistance we came,
When she toiled to emblazon the Conqueror's fame;
And the lasting memorials we are seen,
In a summer clime, of a swarthier queen.

The records of ancient days we bear,
And Time to erase us doth not dare,
Yet the poorest girl in our native land
Hath held us fast in her weary hand.

We steadily turn from the tropical glow
To the dreary regions of ice and snow,
For we're firmly bound with a magic spell,
Which none may loose, or its meaning tell.

Woe to the man who hath dared to wed
A woman who us and our use hath fled!
If you find us out, you may claim to be
As bright and as sharp as ever are we!

Enigma No. 2.

A whimsical set we must often seem,
Of crotchets as full as an organist's dream;
If we were abolished, there'd straightway be
A piscatorian jubilee.

We are frequently clothed in a snowy array
As a maiden fair on her bridal day;
Yet we're often black as the blackest night,
E'en when we're lauding the soft moonlight.
The depths of the ocean we faithfully show;
On us hundreds of miles you may swiftly go;
We measure the distance from place to place,
And encircle the globe in our wide embrace.
Woe, woe to the soldier who dares to fly
From us when the hour of battle is nigh!
Yet the gardener himself, in his peaceful trade,
For planting his cabbages needs our aid.
If a lady endeavours her age to hide,
We ruthlessly publish it far and wide
Wherever she ventures to show her head;
Yet in us her destiny oft is read.
In the heart of a friend long, long forsaken
A few of ourselves may deep gladness awaken,
Yet ours is a many-stringed, changeful lyre,
For dismay and despair we may often inspire.
We're essential to poets, to artists, musicians,
To all washerwomen, and mathematicians;
It required a Euclid to tell what we be,
Yet us at this moment, fair reader, you see.

Enigma No. 3.

I AM a native of many a land,
Of Norway's forests, of India's strand;
And beautiful England's smiles and tears
Have ripened and watered my early years.
I am found near the lowliest cottage fire,
And I dwell in the solemn cathedral choir,
The royal hall I am sure to grace,
And always in Parliament find a place;
Around me oft gather the great of the land,
In front of the Queen I audaciously stand;
And Arthur himself, in days of yore,
Owed half his renown to me or more.

As a quadruped oftenest I have been,
One-legged, or three-footed, or legless I'm seen.
The schoolboy I help through his hard calculation
When working a question in multiplication.
Since the era of Moses (who, truth to speak,
In a manner unfitting his character meek,
Most shamefully used me), till quite of late,
I've always been sober, and still, and sedate;
But now I am playing such wondrous vagaries,
That whether Beelzebub, witches, or fairies,
Electric attraction, or galvanic power,
Have thus turned my head, up to this present hour,
The wisest and cleverest brains of the day,
Quite out of their depth, are unable to say.
In olden days to my care were confided
The laws by which monarchs and subjects were guided;
The records of feats of chivalry,
Or of deeds of blood, were preserved by me:
But now having leaves, though, alas! no flower,
I bear what must pass in a single hour.

Enigma No. 4.

Of a useful *whole* I'm the most useful part;
I've a good circulation, for I've a heart;
I have two or three garments or outer clothes;
I am closely allied to a lip and nose;
Rags, and parchments, and jewels rare,
Rubbish and treasures within me I bear;
The tiniest leaf I produce I can nip
With a dexterous finger and thumb at my tip;
Though I'm often as tall as a spire to view,
If you travel far I accompany you;
I am the Indian's light canoe:
To puzzle you more, I'm an aquaduct too;
I'm part of a garment of olden time,
And part of a beast of a southern clime;
And finally, now, to crown the whole,
I am your body, but not your soul!

Enigma No. 5.

A TERM for autumn leaves when all their lovely tints are fled;
A mountain in Arabia, lifting high its rocky head;
What witches and astrologers pretend they truly are;
A state from which I greatly hope your conscience still is far:
Those four are all alike, you'll see, in mere pronunciation,
But diverse in orthography and in signification.
Transpose the second, you will gain the title of a king,
And what you would be sure to do if he should enter in;
Transpose the fourth, you'll see at once how ancient warriors treated
The cities of the enemy, with passion overheated;
Transpose the third, and lo! the first will straightway be revealed.
Now, reader, I shall like to see this mystery unsealed.

Enigma No. 6.

SEVENTEEN hundred and sixty yards,
A maiden's name and a term at cards,
A halting leg, something stronger than beer,
A river to many a student dear,
A fragrant tree, and a foreign fruit,
A government coach on a postal route,
Honiton, Brussels, or Valenciennes,
A spice preceding bishops and deans,
A sin of the tongue, and the stronger sex,
The state of the sea when no tempests vex,
What you look for three or four times a day,
What the Prince of Wales to the crown will lay,
Three Scripture names, and a region wide,
What an archer takes his shaft to guide:
With six little letters all these are framed;
When each you have duly and rightly named,
They form what I hope you will never dare
Against friend or foe in your heart to bear.

Enigma No. 7.

IF you get into me, I have no sort of doubt,
But that you will endeavour forthwith to get out;
Behead me, and then I'm the lone widow's weeds;
Behead me again, and I'm tiny round seeds;
Repeat yet again the above operation,
And I am renowned for my quick imitation,
My mischievous habits, and horrid grimaces,—
You're myself, if you practise unnatural graces.

Enigma No. 8.

WHAT was I? Such a clever friar,
I barely 'scaped the witches' pyre;
Yet doth philosophy in me
One of her bright admirers see;
And forms of classic beauty grew
Beneath my hand to nature true;
Each wondrous magic lantern show
To me the happy children owe;
With Schwartz contesting, I should mention
The honour of his great invention.
What am I? What you may despise,
For I am little more than grease,
And yet I am an annual prize
For matrimonial love and peace.
In every scrape or awkward plight
I hope to save me you'll be able.
I am the ploughboy's great delight,
And often grace his Sunday table.
From dreams of mire and sweet repose
To streaky excellence I rose;
And, following still the chimney sweep,
I learned to smoke instead of sleep.

Enigma No. 9.

In fiery caverns was my glowing birth,
The great laboratories of the earth;
Thence issuing, with devastating power,
Entombing cities in a single hour;
The vineyards of bright Sicily have been
Of my o'erwhelming might too oft the dreary scene.

Yet I encircle many a fair white arm,
Or holding ink and pens give no alarm;
Though none may stay my incandescent course
Till Neptune doth oppose his briny force.
Mysterious child of subterranean fires,
Strange relics I preserve of fair Italia's sires.

Enigma No. 10.

The royal sun with his orbèd flame
To be myself I modestly claim;
And yet, though strange, it is perfectly true,
I am at this moment within your shoe.
Have you a delicate hand to show?
Its symmetry partly to me you owe;
And I cannot think how you can possibly see
If deprived in another part of me.
The ancient dame, with her spectacled nose,
By my strange contortions I often pose,
As I glide away from her busy hand
To rejoice the juvenile feline band.
I am a being of direful power,
And many I haste to their last dread hour;
Yet the tiny child on his feeble feet
Is gladdened and charmed by my motions fleet.
I am said to whistle, though not to sigh;
Merriment often to hundreds I bring.
On due inquiry I think you will find
That twenty people in me have dined;
Yet when at dinner you take your seat
I'm sometimes the very first thing you eat.

Who patronise me? The college youth,
Loving me better than books in truth;
The friends of science, the friends of strife,
The duellist seeking his fellow's life,
Of sharpers and blacklegs not a few,
Equine doctors frequently too,
The conjuror showing his skilful tricks,
In the list the graceful and fair we mix;
And last, not least, our gracious Queen
My patroness certainly ever hath been.

Enigma No. 11.

I AM a reward, and a punishment too,
What you may give, and what you may do,
Animal, mineral, both I may be,
Vegetable oftenest perhaps of the three.
Once, I know, as the story goes,
I was the cause of a bridegroom's woes;
But often since I have dimmed the life
Of a wearily-sighing neglected wife.
Never a court without me was seen,
Never a vestry either, I ween,
Never a coach, and never a train,
Tho' sometimes a hindrance the latter to gain.
Famous I am for a long dark way,
Dismal as night in the brightest day.
From the depths of my bosom may rise and float
Many a soft and melodious note;
Why should ye marvel? The rich and fair,
The gay and gorgeous are often there.
Wherever the sweetest of sounds goes forth
Through the radiant south or the dreary north,
A tale of me will be surely told,
Or false were the words of a prophecy old.
A little one longs to begin to do good,
I sometimes help it; and always could;
Yet the hardened man and the cruel boy
May find in me a savage joy.

Give me, and oh, what a monster you'll be;
Refuse me, "was e'er such a niggard as he";
Hire me, then you are rich, I conclude;
Mount me, and then you may view and be viewed;
Open me, perhaps you are even a thief,
Perhaps 'twas by way of consoling your grief;
Plant me, I see you are neat in your taste;
Enter me—nervousness, flurry, and haste
Won't at all suit, so I pray you take heed,
Or counsel will into me put you indeed.

Enigma No. 12.

Lives there a poet, old or young,
    Who has not sung my praise?
For ever silent be his tongue,
    Forgotten be his lays!

I have a father dark and stern,
    A daughter bright and gay;
I weep upon his funeral urn,
    I die beneath her sway.

And yet that father binds me fast,
    Hushing my low sweet voice;
That daughter sets me free at last,
    And bids me still rejoice.

Deceitful I am said to be,
    A thing of treacherous smiles,
And many meet their end in me,
    Wreck'd by my sunny wiles.

Yet health and cure 'tis mine to give
    To many a sickly frame;
An antelope of Africa
    Usurps my well-known name.

I'm born beneath the cold hard ground,
    Yet life and joy I bring,
With song and mirth to all around,
    Upon my emerald wing.

I help to measure Time's swift flight;
Tide has to do with me;
In guns and traps behold my might:
O say what can I be?

Enigma No. 13.

That I'm very well-known to all metaphysicians 'tis true,
Whose brains I attempted to clear, being one of the crew;
A secret of wonderful power in me was conceal'd,
Which firstly by love, but by treachery next was revealed;
I never am mentioned as living, though oft in the city,
When said to be dead, much impatience I rouse, but no pity;
To some navigation I lend indispensable hand,
Yet I'm not of the slightest utility saving inland.
I frequently act as a guardian, though I must own
My wards to attain their majority never were known;
The brow of the maiden to me owes the half of its charms,
And yet, strange to say, I'm a part of death-dealing firearms.
I've a slim coadjutor who with me my secret possesses,
My master he is, for he knows all my inmost recesses;
My safety and faithfulness vanish if once one can gain him,
Yet I'm perfectly useless without him, so prithee retain him.
The apple Eve gathered was never supposed to be me,
And yet if you pick me, beware of the powers that be;
By a figure of speech I'm said to be silver or golden,
Though to metals far baser I really am much more beholden.
Of loved ones far distant I'm often the fondly kept token,
Memorial and echo of harpstrings which death had long broken.

Enigma No. 14.

I may be tall, and slender, and round,
Or perfectly square, and as flat as the ground;
No edifice ever without me is raised,
And yet, when 'tis finished, I never am praised.

The bears themselves, with a grim delight,
Hail me as an old acquaintance quite;

And a smaller quadruped lays its claim
With a feline addition to bear my name.

Glows there a heart in the English breast
Which beats for the injured and long oppressed?
At the thought of me it will rise and swell;
For each free-soul'd patriot knows me well.

Where may you find me? In sunny Kent,
Where the hop-pickers sing, while on labour intent
Or in realms of ice and eternal snow,
'Neath the gorgeous aurora's crimson glow.

In celestial regions I'm certainly found,
And wherever on earth there's an acre of ground;
Where his lordship's chariot proudly speeds,
I ever am close to the high-bred steeds.

I have stood very near to the triple crown,
Yet I'm seen in the back streets of every town;
On the festal day of a short-lived queen
The chief attraction I've ever been.

Attraction, said I? You little know
How much to my power of attraction you owe!
All the gold, and the pearls, the silk, sugar, and tea
That are borne to your homes o'er the pathless sea.

I may quietly stand by your drawing-room fire,
Bearing a comfort you often desire!
Or stretch my bold arm o'er the surging wave,
Some wretch from its billowy depths to save.

Enigma No. 15.

Where will ye seek me? The Andes rise
　　Silently grand beneath tropical skies;
　　And far Himalaya's crowns of snow
Gleam o'er the burning plains below;

Enigma No. 15.

I dwell with each, for the mountain air
Certainly suits me everywhere.
Know ye the silent and death-like realm,
Where winter hath donn'd his glassy helm,
And conquering rules o'er land and sea?
Beneath his throne is the home for me.
Ye may seek in the gay and brilliant throng,
Where the hours fleet by in dance and song;
There, martyr-like, I'm sure to be,
Though to venture there may be death to me.
Yet I'm never afraid of catching cold
(Like some young ladies) however bold.
'Tis a wonder my mother should let me go,
But she is remarkably yielding, I know;
And many who tried us both can say,
She yields directly when I give way.
My character's quite the more solid, I state,
But she is a person of greater weight.
Though never convicted of any crime
'Tis perfectly true that, for months at a time,
I am starved in a dungeon all damp and bare,
With hardly the half of a prisoner's fare.
I'm rather a traveller, I may tell,
And know the Atlantic routes quite well;
Sometimes on my own account I go,
Sometimes whether I will or no.
When will ye seek me? The sultry glow
Of a summer noon is the time, I trow,
When the burning pavement and dusty street
Make you long for a rest for your aching feet.
I have done in my time some wonderful things;
Have been made the dwelling-place of kings;
Have baffled the general's proud careering;
Have outdone Stephenson's engineering.
I nevertheless can condescend
To Monsieur Soyer my aid to lend;
Or, better still, can bring mirth and joy
To the heart of the sturdy village boy.

Enigma No. 16.

    Primeval woods my parent's birth
    Beheld, where no loud axe was heard,
    Where through a solitary earth
    No voice the leafy echoes stirred;
But I was born in gloominess profound,
In sable swaddling clothes the child of light was bound.

    Released at length by human skill,
    From long confinement forth I sped,
    And in each city's highway still
    I linger far beneath your tread;
Though there are times when, grovelling thus no more,
Beyond the clouds of earth, a prisoner still, I soar.

    No eye my subtle form may see,
    Till, coming forth to light,
    A slow consumption wasteth me
    In man's unpitying sight.
Yet when from durance vile I swift escape,
All feel my baleful presence, though none see my shape.

    I smile upon the giddy scene
    Of mirth, and revelry, and song;
    Yet in the sacred courts have been
    Devotion's handmaid long;
With darkness waging constant strife and sure,
I ever shun the day-beams though so bright and pure.

    Though none have ever heard my voice,
    Yet words of gladness traced in me
    Have bid full many a heart rejoice,
    When England's flag waved high and free.
And with the song of victory sweetly blended
The full deep hymn of praise that war's dark storm was ended.

Enigma No. 17.

    I am the child of the brightest thing
    Which may gladden mortal eyes,

Yet the silent sweep of my dusky wing
Over my mother may dimness fling,
   And smiling she faints and dies.

I move, I dance, I fall, I fly,
   Yet anon I may calmly sleep;
I mark the bright-winged hours flit by,
Your ingenuity perhaps I try;
   I am long, or short, or deep.

I have been hailed as a boon untold,
   Or dreaded and shunned ere now;
The earth in my wide embrace I fold,
The mountain regions are my stronghold,
   Yet I steadily follow the plough.

I may rest a while in the minster pile,
   Or beneath the old oak tree;
Often with trackless step I pass
O'er the whispering corn and the waving grass,
   Or tread the changeful sea.

All the day through I follow you,
   Yet beware how you follow me;
For each child of man I may oft beguile,
And cloud the light of his sunniest smile,
   Till for ever away I flee.

Enigma No. 18.

Ye have seen me in the skies,
Yet beneath the ground I rise:
Sometimes far above your head,
Sometimes deep below your tread.

Where the forest boughs entwine,
Baffling still the gay sunshine;
Gaze aloft, and you will see
In myself their tracery.

Laughing eye and dimpling smile
May be even me awhile;
Playful words, like javelins thrown,
As myself you often own.

Many a sunny stream ye trace,
Rippling in my calm embrace;
Still I watch the secret shrine
Of the rich and ruddy wine.

Nave, and choir, and aisle, I trow,
All to me their glories owe;
Even a seraph form by me,
Greater, fairer yet may be.

Many a loved one may be laid
In my sadly solemn shade;
On your brow I now may dwell,
While your lips my name will tell.

Enigma No. 19.

Say, know ye not the pilgrim band,
    Who wander far and wide,
And greeting find in every land
    Wherever they abide?

They meet full many a friend I wot,
    Who fain would have them stay;
To such they cling, and leave them not,
    Yet still go on their way.

Each bears a staff and often twain,
    And need they many a rest;
The oldest oft seems young again,
    And perhaps we love them best.

They speak a language passing sweet,
    With heart-lore richly fraught;
But oh! to some they daily meet
    Their eloquence is nought.

Yet strange the laws their speech obeys,
    Who drink its mystic tone
May find within each simplest phrase
    A meaning all their own.

Some deem they tell of long past years,
    When they were girls and boys;
Some only hear of bygone tears,
    And some of present joys.

Some hear them speak of One who sent
    That welcome pilgrim band,
And bless the love that freely lent
    Such boon to every land.

Enigma No. 20.

OH, haughty Thebes! In shadowy days of yore,
Where history faintly blends with mythologic lore,
I was thy hidden terror, yet, revealed,
I traced a stain of woe upon thy glittering shield.

Fair Palestine! I was put forth in thee
Amid a scene of gay festivity;
Yet brought by me a sullen frown, I ween,
Was on the brow of my originator seen.

'Tis mine to give thee strange and needless toil,
For Gordian knots I weave in many a tangled coil
I shun publicity, for I declare,
That if you speak my name, I vanish into air.

Enigma No. 21.

THOUGH constantly we're in the mire,
We shine and sparkle with our fire;
Part of the verb " to speak " we need,
And yet no words from us proceed.
The annals of the Inquisition
Reveal too well our awful mission;

In what they call the "good old days,"
Our patronesses won high praise.
It is our business to convey
Men, beasts, and chattels day by day;
You often bear us near your heart,
And would be loth from us to part.
Though never weary with our speed,
Full often we are tired indeed;
A tribe of insects, most minute,
Receive from us a name to suit.
Long since we used to condescend
Our aid in cookery to lend.
We guide the vessel in its course,
And multiply your puny force.

Charade No. 1.

THE veiling shades of night departed,
    On Lebanon's heights was a rosy glow,
When the serried ranks of the Lion-hearted
    Prepared for my *first* at the Moslem foe.
A voice was heard, like a clarion proud,
    Forth, forth to battle, to glory go!
To my lovely *second* I solemnly vowed
    To crush the insolent Moslem foe.
And forth they went, but the voice was stilled,—
    A stroke of my *whole* had laid him low;
By other hands was the vow fulfilled,
    For they tamed the pride of the Moslem foe.

Charade No. 2.

MY *first* gleams bright 'mid azure shields,
On rich emblazoned argent fields.
If you too often use my *second*,
An egotist you will be reckoned.
My *third*, it is a battle-cry;
And be it yours in every high,

And good, and noble end and aim,
As such it is the road to fame.
My belted *whole* you may descry
Illumining the southern sky.

Charade No. 3.

FROM his ruby pavilion Phœbus arose,
    And looked down from his shining *first,*
And the earth at his glance, from her calm repose
    Into beauty and gladness burst,
But the clouds of sorrow he could not chase,
Nor the gleaming tears upon Katie's face.

On a merry ride to the busy town
    In my *first* she too surely had reckoned,
Disappointed and angry she flung herself down
    On my *whole:* but alas, in my *second;*
So I told her, my *second* you never can be
While such haughty tempers so often I see.

Charade No. 4.

HURRAH for merry England!
    For good Saint George hurrah!
For Richard of the Lion Heart,
    The noble and the gay,
Returns from long captivity,
    And 'tis a festal day.

With chivalry and minstrelsy
    The hours shall speed along,
Where meet the beauteous and the brave,
    The gentle and the strong.
(I would my *first* had gazed upon
    The gladly loyal throng.)

The warriors of Palestine,
    Who led my *second* well

When on the ranks of Saladin
    Like avalanche they fell,
Now in the tournament alone
    A fancied foe repel.

The Saxon serf may lay aside
    His clumsy *third,* I trow;
And leave it in the silent field,
    With cool and sweatless brow;
For what has he to do to-day
    With weary spade and plough?

But who is he, the Saxon youth,
    With royal Saxon bride,
Who Saracen and Templar hath
    Successfully defied?
He is my famous *whole,* I ween,
    The valiant and the tried.

Charade No. 5.

My *second* could never produce my *first,*
Though its opposite frequently may;
'Tis a thing that's trampled upon and cursed,
So tell me its name, I pray.

In my *whole* both my *second* and *first* you would see,
With more of the latter than pleasant;
A treat I consider this latter to be,
Though, like all earthly good, evanescent.

Above my *second* 'tis commonly borne,
Though carefully kept below it;
Full many a home it has caused to mourn,
And the newspaper accidents show it.

When my *second* is looking its dullest and worst,
And my *whole* must be dreary indeed,
Like a hard-hearted tyrant comes forth my *first,*
With whom it were vain to plead.

Charade No. 6.

Where the tall pine-forest made
Deepest, darkest, holiest shade,
Came Nesota, sorrow-laden,
She, the lovely Indian maiden.
Came, ere she had waited long,
Karanò, the swift, the strong;
He, who bowed to nought beside,
Bent to her in lowly pride;
Bent, until his lofty brow,
Loftiest of the tribes around,
Touched the greensward hallowed now,
Where her *first* had kissed the ground.

"Karanò! arise and fly!
Hands of power and wrath are nigh,
From thy side shall I be driven,
Like a willow lightning-riven.
Karanò, ere thou depart,
Lay this *second* on thy heart,
Token of Nesota's love,
From thy own, thy stricken dove."
Trembling in his hand she laid
My shining *second,* then farewell!
She is gone, through bush and blade,
Fleetly as a wild gazelle.

Karanò, the swift, the strong,
Baffles all pursuers long,
Till the moon is on the wane;
Then a red deer they have slain.
To the treacherous banquet led,
When the new moon's feast is spread,
They have mingled in his bowl,
Secretly, my deadly *whole.*
Karanò hath found repose
Where my *whole* doth darkly wave,
And the tall pine-forests close
O'er Nesota's quiet grave.

Charade No. 7.

My *whole*, the poet of flood and fell,
   Of valley and breezy hill,
Has passed from the scenes he loved so well,
   And none his place may fill.
In his *first*, with their simple and childlike grace,
   Of his *second* an index all may trace.

Charade No. 8.

Soon the hour of dawn shall pass,
   Clear and loud the lark is singing;
Swiftly through the waving grass
   Now my bright-eyed *first* is springing.

Down the still and shadowy dale
   Floats my *second*, sweetly telling,
" Morning lifts her misty veil,
   Spectral darkness soon dispelling."

Far remote from beaten way,
   Now my dewy *whole* is bending;
And where summer breezes play
   Sweetness to their breath is lending.

Charade No. 9.

Distant from the noisy town
   Sits my *first* and *next* alone,
In my ivy-wreathen *whole*,
   Loved and blessed by many a soul.

More than on my *first*, I ween,
   With his brethren he hath been;
But my *third* hath touched his brow,
   And he waits in silence now;

Hoping soon to see the day
When his *second*, far away,

May replace his trembling voice:
This shall make his *third* rejoice.

Charade No. 10.

My *first* dwells in the torrid zone,
    Its beauty and its boon,
Yet this the Esquimaux must own
    Beneath an Arctic moon.

He who would do it is untrue,
    Though all in every land
To bear it off in strife desire,
    It always is at hand.

My *first* and *next* in days of yore
    Went forth in lowly guise:
A staff was theirs, but little store
    Of what the world would prize.

Yet one, alas! in later days,
    With murder on his brow,
Revealed how far in guilty ways
    A child of earth may go.

My *last* I think you'll quickly name
    In half a minute more;
Are twenty hundreds quite the same
    As just a hundred score?

For if you say what each would be,
    The name you will have got;
And yet, reversing, you will see
    That surely it is *not*.

My *whole* I leave without debate,
    For 'tis not woman's mission
To criticise the wise and great
    And play the politician.

Charade No. 11.

Awake, ye sleepers!
My *first* hath sung his loud reveille,
And wakened through the glistening dale
    The early reapers.

Why will ye linger?
Is it no *second* that ye hear
The morning hymn, so glad and clear,
    Of that wise singer?

Come forth, nor tarry!
And track the busy-wingèd bee,
Who from my *whole* right joyously
    Sweet spoil doth carry.

Charade No. 12.

Arise, my *first*! In peerless radiance beaming,
A veil of glory thou dost weave for earth:
The ocean waves to welcome thee are gleaming,
For thou alone to Beauty givest birth.

Shine forth, my *second*! Freshly now is flowing
The busy stream of life, and labour too;
Each heart with ardour, base or noble glowing,
Till thou shalt close, arresting all they do.

All hail, my *whole*! thou comest with rich pleasure
An angel from the land of pure delight,
The great man's blessing, and the poor man's treasure,
Our earnest of the day which knows no night.

Charade No. 13.

My *first* had spread her darksome wing
O'er all the loveliness of spring;
My *third* arose with mournful wail—
The young leaves told their first sad tale,
The old oak groaned, the flowerets sighed,
The hawthorn bloom was scattered wide:

But ere my gloomy *first* had passed,
When silent was my *third* at last,
My *whole* awoke the moonlight dell
To list the sweet tale she could tell;
Then mingled, in strange harmony,
Silence and sweetest melody.
"Your *second*, why such strange omission?"
'Tis but a tiny preposition.

Charade No. 14.

HEARD ye the long, low roar
Blend with the sea-mew's cry?
Saw ye the nearing shore
Where the white foam-wreaths lie?
O wait, seaman, wait while the tempest shall last,
For my *first* is a danger thou hast not passed.

How shall the seaman wait?
There stands his white-walled home,
From its blithely opened gate
Never more need he roam.
My *second* he brings from a distant realm,
And leaves he for ever the weary helm.

On! for the tide ebbs fast!
On! for the night grows dark,
But the cold wave-arms are cast
Round the seaman's sinking bark.
He makes my *whole* with the angry sea,—
Thine be the gold, so my life go free!

Charade No. 15.

My *whole* is but a species of my *third*,
Yet has my *third* no right to such a name
Unless my *first and second* form a word,
To which he lays an undisputed claim;
But if my *whole* renounce my *first* and *second*,
My *first* indeed he may, but not my *whole*, be reckoned.

Charade No. 16.

THE all-victorious Roman
　　Hath raised his eagles high,
The Carthaginian foeman
　　Right proudly to defy.

Forth marched in noble daring
　　The leader of the day,
A mighty *second* bearing
　　In all the stern affray.

Ye glorious ranks, assemble!
　　"Push on, my *first*," he cried,
"And soon their *whole* shall tremble,
　　And crushed shall be their pride."

Charade No. 17.

ENTER my *first* with a studied grace,
Conceit in his head, and a smirk on his face;
Of fashion he deems himself quite the top,
And he's scented like any perfumer's shop;
So among the ladies he's surely reckoned,
For the evening at least, to be quite my *second*.
But oh! what a fall for the brilliant star!
A lady's whisper is heard too far:
"Of all the flowers that ever were,
The only one I to him compare
Is my scentless *whole,* with its gaudy stare."
Not quite rightly spelt, but comparison rare.

[This was the end of the original book, *Streamlets of Song for the Young.*]

> *Arithmetical Enigma.*
> 5/12 of the square of 3/5 of a score,
> 1/8 of a dozen & 1/2 of one more,
> 2/5 of 1/4 of 5/9 of eighteen,
> Of 25, 20, & 12 take the mean,
> 4/15 of 5/6 of 9/10 of one-third
> Of 120, will give you a word
> Which in literal truth, I will fearlessly state
> Must form the foundation of everything great.
>
> N.B. The initials of the above numbers form the answer.

Two copies of the "Arithmetical Enigma" were found, both very clear copies in F.R.H.'s handwriting: this one was found on a separate piece of paper, and the other manuscript was found on page 20 of her Manuscript Book № IV (on page 88 of this book). The fact that two copies were found, and that Frances wrote the complete poem in her Manuscript Book, demonstrates that she regarded this as a finalized poem to be kept and included. As explained on the next page, both copies had the mistake of 1/8 instead of the correct 1/3.

Arithmetical Enigma

5/12 of the square of 3/5 of a score,
1/3 of a dozen and 1/2 of one more,
2/5 of 1/4 of 5/9 of eighteen,
Of 25, 20, and 12 take the mean,
4/15 of 5/6 of 9/10 of one-third
Of 120, will give you a word
Which in <u>literal</u> truth, I will fearlessly state,
Must form the foundation of everything great.

N.B.[1] The initials of the above numbers form the answer.

[1] N.B.: *nota bene*—Latin, "note well."

Note: In the hand-written manuscript of the Arithmetical Enigma, Frances mistakenly wrote 1/8 at the beginning of line 2, and she almost certainly meant 1/3. (When I did the arithmetic, 1/8 makes the answer to line 2 seven and a half. Later I realized that she almost certainly meant to write 1/3. Haydn once wrote above a mistake in a manuscript score he composed, "written in my sleep.") Possibly Maria V. G. Havergal and Frances Anna Shaw did not realize the mistake, could not solve the Enigma, and thus might have thought that it should not be published. The Arithmetical Enigma is a brilliant poem: the arithmetic is simple (very accessible to children), but the words to make the poem, and the ideas, are brilliant.   David Chalkley

Solution to the Arithmetical Enigma on page 705:
    3/5 times 20 equals 60/5. That is twelve.
    12 squared is 144.
    5/12 times 144 equals 720/12. That is sixty.
        The answer to line one is sixty.   S

1/3 of a dozen is 4. Half of another dozen is 6. 4 plus 6 equals 10.
    The answer to line two is ten.   T

2/5 times 1/4 equals 2/20. That is 1/10.
1/10 times 5/9 equals 5/90.
5/90 times 18 equals 90/90. That is one.
    The answer to line three is one.   O

25 plus 20 plus 12 equal 57.
57 divided by 3 equals 19.
    The answer to line four is nineteen.   N

The fifth and sixth lines combine to be one answer.
4/15 times 5/6 equals 20/90.
20/90 times 9/10 equals 180/900. That is 1/5.
1/5 times 1/3 equals 1/15.
1/15 times 120 equals 120/15. That is 8.
    The answer to lines 5 and 6 is eight.   E

STONE

Note: All the Engimas and all the Charades (plus an additional Charade, No. 18, "Gladstone") were published in the definitive edition *The Poetical Works of Frances Ridley Havergal,* edited by Maria V. G. Havergal and Frances Anna Shaw (London: James Nisbet & Co., 1884). This collection of poems by F.R.H. for children, *Streamlets of Song for the Young* (London: James Nisbet & Co., 1887), was compiled and edited by her oldest sister, Jane Miriam Havergal Crane. The answers to all the Enigmas are the same in both volumes (given with the titles on the Contents pages, on pages 4-5 of this book). There is a difference in the answers for four of the Charades between the earlier volume (*The Poetical Works of Frances Ridley Havergal*) and this volume of Miriam's *Streamlets of Song for the Young.*

Charade	*The Poetical Works,* 1884	*Streamlets of Song for the Young,* 1887
No. 2.	Orion.	Carpet.
No. 3.	Carpet.	Orion.
No. 12.	Sunday.	Nightingale.
No. 13.	Nightingale.	Sunday.

To this reader (David Chalkley), the correct answers to these four Charades seem more likely to be the answers in the 1884 *Poetical Works,* and the answers in the 1887 *Streamlets* seem more likely to be mistakes.

Miriam did not include Charade No. 18 by Frances ("Gladstone"), apparently finding it too adult for children to decipher. Because this is included (as the final Charade) in *The Poetical Works of Frances Ridley Havergal,* this Charade is given here.

Charade No. 18.

A BRIGHT and joyous frame of mind,
With Cephas properly combined,
Produce, I'll boldly dare to say,
A statesman of the present day.

This next, single verse was found among Havergal manuscripts and papers. Written by Frances, this was apparently a Charade not published with the other 18 Charades. [No answer was found with this.}

Say, is not my <u>whole</u> a prize,
While my <u>first</u> it gratifies,
And my <u>second</u> 'tis indeed,
Bright with many a dewy bead.

An undated photograph of Frances Ridley Havergal. See also page 134.

F. R. H.'s Thanks.

*With a copy of "Songs of Grace and Glory," to Clara O.,
for thirty bunches of Astley violets.*

SWEET flowers of Spring,
   All fresh and fair to see,
      You sent to me;
Sweet holy " Songs of Grace
      And Glory," too,
      I send to you.

Grace all-sufficient may
      You find, and know
      On earth below,
Till God's own glory crown
      Your faith and love,
      In heaven above.

Inscription in a Copy of "Life's Morning."

BY Him "Life's *Morning*" lovelit be,
Who loved, and lived and died for thee:
So shall thy *Noontide* never know
Earth's burning thirst, or withering glow:
And thou shalt fear no gathering night;
At *Eventide* it shall be light.

The Disappointed Carol Singers.

OH, must we not sing our Christmas hymn,
   And will you not hear our song?
With joyous voice, but with weary limb,
   We have roamed the whole day long!

We have thought of the merry Christmas time
   For many a week before,
And have gleefully learnt our Christmas rhyme
   To carol at your door.

There are no merry larks to wake you now,
    No blackbirds in woody dell;
The nightingale loves not the leafless bough,
    The humming bee sleeps in his cell.

Oh, winter is gloomy and dark enough,
    And must it be silent too?
Are the chorus of winds and the storm-song rough
    The only sweet music for you?

But we are the birds of the winter day,
    When all else is dark and still;
Then, lady, send us not all away,
    And with sorrow our eager hearts fill.

Oh, do not thus wave your beautiful hand,
    And bid us unheard to go;
For the carolling time of our little band
    Comes but once a year, you know.

Welcome to Winterdyne.

FRANCIE and Willie, welcome to you!
    Alfred and Alice, welcome too!
To an English home and English love
Welcome, each little Irish dove!
Never again we hope to be
Kept apart by an angry sea.
A thousand welcomes, O darlings mine,
    When we see you at Winterdyne!

Welcome all to a warm new nest,
    Just the place for our doves to rest,
Through the oaks and beeches looking down
On the winding valley and quaint old town,
Where ivy green on the red rock grows,
And silvery Severn swiftly flows,
With an extra sparkle and glitter and shine
    Under the woods of Winterdyne.

On a quiet evening in lovely spring,
    In the tall old elms the nightingales sing;
Under the forest in twilight grey,
I have heard them more than a mile away,
Sweeter and louder and far more clear
Than any thrush you ever did hear;
Perhaps, when the evenings grow long and fine,
    They will sing to you in Winterdyne.

Little to sadden, and nothing to fear;
    Priest and Fenian never come here;
Only the sound of the Protestant bells
Up from the valley pleasantly swells,
And a beautiful arch, to church, is made
Under the sycamore avenue's shade;
You pass where its arching boughs entwine,
    Out of the gates of Winterdyne.

Welcome to merry old England! And yet
    We know that old Ireland you will not forget;
Many a thought and prayer will fly
Over the mountains of Wales so high,
Over the forest and over the sea,
To the home which no longer yours must be.
But farewells are over, O darlings mine,
    Now it is Welcome to Winterdyne!

To Jericho and Back.

Suggested by a child's remark, "What a queer place Jericho must be, if all the persons and things get there that are *wished* there!"

ONCE on a time I a visit had paid,
All very pleasant as long as I made
Remarks on the topics I fancied or guessed
Any one present was sure to like best.
Then came the trial of courage and skill;—
(Oh for a talent for gilding the pill!)
Out of my pocket with tremulous thought
A card for collecting was cautiously brought.

What the result, there is no need to tell;
Collectors are often received very well,
Sometimes, alas! it is quite the reverse,
So you take up the work for better, for worse;
Still, I was conscious 'twas better to go
After revealing my errand, and so
Forth in the mist of the evening I wandered,
And on changes of tone and of countenance
    pondered!

Weary the feet, and closing the day;
Is there not danger of losing the way?
Strange are the hills and the forests around;
Where shall a home-leading pathway be found?
I cannot turn back, and I cannot advance; —
Is it a nightmare, or is it a trance?
Shadowy figures are faintly seen,
Spectral and silent, dimly serene;
Persons and things in range on range,
All familiar, yet all so strange;
Shades of all things that ever annoyed,
All that ever one wished to avoid.

Strange though it be, I need not fear;
'Tis a wonderful region, and how I came here
I cannot explain, but as it is so,
Let me investigate whether or no,
And enumerate some of the objects I find;
No names shall be mentioned, so no one will mind.

Determining thus, I quickly began
Everything round me more closely to scan,
Hoping to make a report of the case
To friends who had never discovered the place;
Having set out on this singular track,
Not in a hurry was I to get back.

Aid unexpected was close to my side,
Soon I perceived an invisible guide,
Only a voice, clear, quiet, and low,
Telling me all that I wanted to know.

People of every age and class
Under review appeared to pass;
Some I recognised perfectly well,
(More of these than I choose to tell!)
Of others I learnt the name and degree
From the bodiless guide who followed me.

There were several sharp little girls
Who had made remarks on chignons and curls,
And dozens and dozens of dreadful boys
With special talents for mischief and noise;
Specimens, too, in greatest variety,
Of every sort of bores of society,—
Boorish bores, and bores polite,
People who stay too late at night,
People who make long morning calls,
People who think of nothing but balls,
People who never a move will make,
People who never a hint can take;
Strong-minded bores, and weak-minded too,
Masculine, feminine, not a few;
People who borrow books to lose,
People who will not wipe their shoes,
People who keep your mind on the rack
Lest some pussy escape from the sack;
Over stupid, and over clever;
People who seem to talk for ever;
People who mutter, and people who drawl,
People who will not talk at all.

There were ledgers and day-books in piles on piles,
And letters and papers in files on files;
Foolscap and parchment, deeds and wills;
And oh, such a mass of unpaid bills!

There was a wonderful heap of slates,
Scribbled all over with sums and dates,
With names of counties and names of towns,
With Latin verbs and German nouns,
Vulgar fractions and multiplication,
And plenty more of the like vexation.

And *finished* was seldom seen;
Many a half-worked cushion and screen,
Many a drawing just half done,
Plenty of things in haste begun;
Soon might Patience and Perseverance
Among this collection effect a clearance.

Now and then throughout my stay
Things arrived in a wholesale way;
Sometimes a house came gliding down,
Sometimes a village or even a town;
Sometimes a borough my eyes would meet,
With candidates, voters, and votes complete;
"But," whispered my guide, " the person who sent it
Was never the man who could represent it."

"The person who sent it! that's not at all clear:
Who has the power to send things here?
What is the power, and how does one use it?
Can any one have it if only they choose it?"
"Every one has it," responded my guide;
"Oft by yourself has the power been tried,
On yourself too, or you would not be here,
In this region of shadows so dismal and drear.
Only a wish is the power that brings
Hither this medley of persons and things;
Only a wish of the opposite kind
Loosens the spell, as you'll presently find.
Some one has wished you farther away,
That is the reason you came here to-day;
Some one may wish you were speedily near,
Then you no longer may stay with us here.
Watch your companions, you'll see at a glance
A few are awake, but most in a trance.
Thousands are sent who never know it,
Editors sending many a poet,
Children sending half their teachers,
Listeners sending half their preachers.
There are some who send their dearest friends

If they happen to cross their private ends,
Or give advice which is good and true,
If it's not the thing that they *wish* to do;
Or to be a little too quick of sight."
(If they never came back, it would serve them right!)

Plenty of music went on meanwhile,
Not in the Handel Festival style!
For hither most people agree to despatch
New violins, with players to match,
Old pianos that rattle and jingle,
Or Broadwood grands that make your ears tingle
With polkas and waltzes four hours a day;
All barrel organs, whatever they play;
All German bands that won't play in tune;
People who practise too late or too soon;
Contraltos that groan, and sopranos that squall,
Basses that bellow, and tenors that bawl.
Suddenly, while these melodious strains
Filled up the measure of puzzles and pains,
Everything faded away from my gaze,
Into the deepening darkness and haze;
All the unbearable chaos of sound
Melted away into silence profound.

How I came back, to this day I don't know,
Only I found myself all in a glow,
Hastening into the parlour to see
If I had kept them all waiting for tea.
Welcoming voices said,—"We were afraid
You with some neighbour the evening had staid;
Your presence is wanted to brighten and cheer;
Where have you been? we were wishing you here!"
"Thanks," cried I; "you have called me away
From a limbo of dreary shades to-day.
May you never the pathway know
Leading away to JERICHO!
Or if you are sent on that dismal track,
May loving wishes soon summon you back!"

My Nest.

My lodging was on the cold rough ground,
    And my pillow a rocky shelf;
And the Poet's Corner was full of dust,
And bits of stick and dead leaves, just
    An emblem of myself!

But lo! I find that some little birds,
    With busy beak and wing,
Have made for me a cosy nest,
The very sort that I like best,
Where I can lie in pleasant rest,
    And twitter, if not sing!

And the Poet's Corner is swept so clean,
    And made so nice and neat,
That really I should feel quite rude,
If I don't, in common gratitude,
Produce some verses on the spot,
And pour them out all fresh and hot,
    For my little birds so sweet.

One Question, Many Answers.

    "What wouldst thou be?"
The question hath wakened wild thoughts in me,
And a thousand responses, like ghosts from their graves,
Arise from my soul's unexplored deep caves,
The echoes of every varying mood
Of a wayward spirit all unsubdued;
The voices which thrill through my inmost breast
May tell me of gladness, but not of rest.
    What wouldst thou be?
'Tis well that the answer is not for me.

    "What wouldst thou be?"
An eagle soaring rejoicingly.

One who may rise on the lightning's wing,
Till our wide, wide world seem a tiny thing;
Who may stand on the confines of boundless space,
And the giant form of the universe trace,
While its full grand harmonies swell around,
And grasp it all with mind profound.
    Such would I be,
Only stayed by infinity.

"What wouldst thou be?"
A bright incarnation of melody.
One whose soul is a fairy lute,
Waking such tones as bid all be mute,
Breathing such notes as may silence woe,
Pouring such strains as make joy o'erflow,
Speaking in music the heart's deep emotion,
Soothing and sweet as the shell of the ocean.
    Such would I be,
Like a fountain of music, all pure and free.

"What wouldst thou be?"
A living blossom of poesy.
A soul of mingled power and light,
Evoking images rare and bright,
Fair and pure as an angel's dream;
Touching all with a heavenly gleam;
And royally claiming from poet-throne
Earth's treasure of beauty as all mine own.
    Such would I be—
My childhood's dream in reality!

"What wouldst thou be?"
A wondrous magnet to all I see.
A spirit whose power may touch and bind
With unconscious influence every mind;
Whose presence brings, like some fabled wand,
The love which a monarch may not command.
As the spring awakens from cold repose
The bloomless brier, the sweet wild rose.
    Such would I be,
With the love of all to encircle me.

"What wouldst thou be?"
A wavelet just rising from life's wide sea.
I would I were once again a child,
Like a laughing floweret on mountains wild;
In the fairy realms of fancy dwelling,
The golden moments for sunbeams selling;
Ever counting on bright to-morrows,
And knowing nought of unspoken sorrows.
    Such would I be,
A sparkling cascade of untiring glee.

"What wouldst thou be?"
A blessing to each one surrounding me;
A chalice of dew to the weary heart,
A sunbeam of joy bidding sorrow depart,
To the storm-tossed vessel a beacon light,
A nightingale song in the darkest night,
A beckoning hand to a far-off goal,
An angel of love to each friendless soul:
    Such would I be.
Oh that *such* happiness were for me!

"What wouldst thou be?"
With these alone were no rest for me.
I would be my Saviour's loving child,
With a heart set free from its passions wild,
Rejoicing in Him and His own sweet ways;
An echo of heaven's unceasing praise,
A mirror here of His light and love,
And a polished gem in His crown above.
    Such would I be,
Thine, O Saviour, and one with Thee!

Making Poetry.

LITTLE one, what are you doing,
    Sitting on the window-seat?
Laughing to yourself, and writing,
Some right merry thought inditing,
    Balancing with swinging feet.

"'Tis some poetry I'm making,
    Though I never tried before:
Four whole lines! I'll read them to you.
Do you think them funny, do you?
    Shall I try to make some more?

"I should like to be a poet,
    Writing verses every day;
Then to you I'd always bring them,
You should make a tune and sing them;
    'T would be pleasanter than play."

Think you, darling, nought is needed
    But the paper and the ink,
And a pen to trace so lightly,
While the eye is beaming brightly,
    All the pretty things we think?

There's a secret,—can you trust me?
    Do not ask me what it is!
Perhaps some day you too will know it,
If you live to be a poet,
    All its agony and bliss.

Poetry is not a trifle,
    Lightly thought and lightly made;
Not a fair and scentless flower,
Gaily cultured for an hour,
    Then as gaily left to fade.

'Tis not stringing rhymes together
    In a pleasant true accord;
Not the music of the metre,
Not the happy fancies, sweeter
    Than a flower-bell, honey-stored.

'Tis the essence of existence,
    Rarely rising to the light;
And the songs that echo longest,
Deepest, fullest, truest, strongest,
    With your life-blood you will write.

With your life-blood. None will know it,
    You will never tell them how.
Smile! and they will never guess it:
Laugh! and you will not confess it
    By your paler cheek and brow.

There must be the tightest tension
    Ere the tone be full and true;
Shallow lakelets of emotion
Are not like the spirit-ocean,
    Which reflects the purest blue.

Every lesson you shall utter,
    If the charge indeed be yours,
First is gained by earnest learning,
Carved in letters deep and burning
    On a heart that long endures.

Day by day that wondrous tablet
    Your life-poem shall receive,
By the hand of Joy or Sorrow;
But the pen can never borrow
    Half the records that they leave.

You will only give a transcript
    Of a life-line here and there,
Only just a spray-wreath springing
From the hidden depths, and flinging
    Broken rainbows on the air.

Still, if you but copy truly,
    'T will be poetry indeed,
Echoing many a heart's vibration,
Rather love than admiration
    Earning as your priceless meed.

Will you seek it? Will you brave it?
    'Tis a strange and solemn thing,
Learning long, before your teaching,
Listening long, before your preaching,
    Suffering before you sing.

My Name[1]

From childish days I never heard
    My own baptismal name;
Too small, too slight, too full of glee
Aught else but "Little Fan" to be,
The stately "Frances" not in me
    Could any fitness claim.

Now, in the crowded halls of life,
    May it be mine to bring
Some gentle stir of the heated air,
Some coolness falling fresh and fair,
    Like a passing angel's wing.

My father's name,—oh how I love
    Its else unwonted look!
For his dear sake right dear I hold
Each letter, changed, as he has told,
Long since from early Saxon mould—
    "The rising of the brook."[2]

Of music, holiness, and love
    That name will always tell,
While sacred chant and anthem rise,
Or mourners live whose deepest sighs
To echoes of a Father's will
He tuned, or child, or grandchild still
    On his bright memory dwell.

But "what the R doth represent,"
    I value and revere;
A diamond clasp it seems to be
On golden chains enlinking me
In loyal love to England's hope,
Bulwark 'gainst infidel and Pope,
    The Church I hold so dear.

---

[1] Suggested by the question, "What does the letter R in your initials (F. R. H.) represent?"
[2] "Heavergill"—the heaving or rising of the brook, or gill.

Three hundred years ago was one
    Who held with stedfast hand
That chalice of the truth of God,
And poured its crystal stream abroad
    Upon the thirsting land.

The moderate, the wise, the calm,
    The learned, brave, and good,[1]
A guardian of the sacred ark,
A burning light in places dark,
For cruel, changeless Rome a mark,
    Our Bishop RIDLEY stood.

The vengeance of that foe nought else
    But fiery doom could still:
Too surely fell the lightning stroke
Upon that noble English oak,
Whose acorn-memory survives
In forest ranks of earnest lives,
    And martyr-souls in will.

Rome offered life for faith laid down:
    Such ransom paid not he!
"As long as breath is in this frame,
My Lord and Saviour Christ His name
And His known truth I'll not deny":
He said (and raised his head on high),
    "God's will be done in me."[2]

He knelt and prayed, and kissed the stake,
    And blessed his Master's name
That he was called His cross to take,
And counted worthy for His sake
    To suffer death and shame.[3]

---

[1] "A man beautified with such excellent qualities, so ghostly inspired and godly learned, and now written doubtless in the book of life with the blessed saints of the Almighty, crowned and throned amongst the glorious company of martyrs."—*Foxe's Acts and Monuments.*

[2] See Works of Bishop Ridley, Parker Society, pp. 295 and 296.

[3] Ibid.

Though fierce the fire and long the pain
    The martyr's God was nigh;
Till from that awful underglow
Of torture terrible and slow,
Above the weeping round about,
Once more the powerful voice rang out
    His Saviour's own last cry.

Oh faithful unto death! the crown
    Was shining on thy brow,
Before the ruddy embers paling,
And sobbing after-gusts of wailing
Had died away, and left in silence
That truest shrine of British Islands,
    That spot so sacred now!

In dear old England shineth yet
    The candle lit that day;
Right clear and strong its flames arise,
Undimmed, unchanged, toward the skies,
By God's good grace it never dies,
    A living torch for aye.

'Tis said that while he calmly stood
    And waited for the flame,
He gave each trifle that he had,
True relic-treasure, dear and sad,
    To each who cared to claim.
I was not there to ask a share,
But reverently for ever wear
    That noble martyr's *name*.

A Song of Welcome.

(For the St. Nicholas Sunday School.)

OH God, with grateful hearts we come
    Thy goodness to adore,
While we our Pastor welcome home
    To England's happy shore.

For Thy delivering love we praise,
    And Thy restoring hand,—
Oh spare him yet for long, long days
    To this our little band.

Thy Spirit's fulness on him rest,
    Thy love his sunshine be!
And may he still, while doubly blest,
    A blessing be from Thee.

When the Chief Shepherd shall appear,
    May he receive, we pray,
A crown of glory bright and clear
    That fadeth not away.

"The Lord is Gracious."

"The Lord is gracious and full of compassion, slow to anger and of great mercy."
—Psalm 145:8.

The Lord is gracious—full of grace
To those who seek through Christ His face;
O come then, sinner, taste and see
The fulness *of His love* for thee.

Full of compassion is His heart,
Each weary sigh, each rankling smart
Is known to Him whom we adore,
The Saviour who our sorrows bore.

To anger slow! though every hour
Provoking His destroying power;
How strange, such words of peace to give,
Through Him who died that we might live.

Great mercy! Yet another seal
To all His gracious words reveal;
Great mercy for the greatly stained,
For those who mercy long disdained.

We little know God's thoughts to man,
They are too great for us to scan:
Thou art too high and we too low,
The wonders of Thy love to know.

But crown Thy mercies, Lord, and send
Thy Spirit as our Teacher-Friend;
That we may see, and feel, and praise
The grace and love of all Thy ways!

In the very fine volume *The Poetical Works of Frances Ridley Havergal* (London: James Nisbet & Co., 1884) prepared by Frances' sister, Maria Vernon Graham Havergal, and their niece (and Frances' god-daughter) Frances Anna Shaw, there is a section of poems entitled "Children's Chords." Seven poems in "Children's Chords" were not included in Miriam's collection *Streamlets of Song for the Young* and are given next. Then in conclusion five further poems are given.

F. R. H.'s Thanks.

For a pencil-case from her Bible-class.

O THOU who gatherest with loving arm
The tender lambs, who in each dark alarm
Wilt fold them safely,—listen to my prayer
Borne upwards on the silent morning air!
O Saviour, e'en to these extend Thy love,
And let them know its sweetness,—from above
Pour down on them Thy Spirit's quickening showers
That they may flourish as sweet heaven-born flowers!
O let Thy smile beam on them, let them be
For ever gladdened with its radiancy!
May they reflect Thine image pure and bright
As burnished silver, spotless in Thy sight;
Cleansed by Thy blood from every sinful stain,
Let not its free stream pour for them in vain.
When Thou in glory at the last Great Day
Shalt come, when earth and heaven shall flee away,
When, waking at the archangel's clarion sound,
The sleeping ones arise, and gather round
The great tribunal, then let each one here
At Thy right hand redeemed and saved appear,
And in the Book of Life let each one be
Inscribed as in eternal lines by Thee!
O Saviour, let *each* name be *written* there,
Not one be wanting in those pages gleaming!
Hear, Shepherd of the lambs, this fervent prayer,
For ever be Thy blessings o'er them streaming!
Another undated photograph of F.R.H. See also page 116.

"Who will take care of me?"

I

"Who will take care of me?" darling, you say,
Lovingly, tenderly watched as you are!
Listen! I give you the answer today,
ONE Who is never forgetful or far.

II

He will take care of you! All through the day
Jesus is near you to keep you from ill;
Walking or resting, at lessons or play,
Jesus is with you & watching you still.

III

He will take care of you! All through the night,
Jesus, the Shepherd, His little one keeps;
Darkness to Him is the same as the light,
He never slumbers & He never sleeps.

IV

He will take care of you! All through the year,
Crowning each day with His kindness & love;
Sending you blessings, & shielding from fear,
Leading you on to the bright home above.

V

He will take care of you! Yes, to the end,
⁴He will not leave you one moment alone.
Darling, be glad that you have such a Friend,
²Nothing can alter His love to His own.

Dayspring. March /73.   Dec: 28. 1872.

F.R.H.'s fair copy autograph of "Who will take care of me?" This poem was started on one page and finished on the next page, in her Manuscript Book Nº VII. She later reversed the order of the second and fourth lines of the last verse. See page 12 of this book.

A mother's loss! Oh who may tell
Its anguish, or what power can quell
The deepest grief, most heartfelt woe
Which childhood's sunny hours may
                      [know.
Ah! childhood's happy days are past
In mirth and glee; no shades are cast
Upon their bright and happy way
Where sunbeams ere around them play.

No cares have they: the floweret sweet
Springs up to cheer their tiny feet.
Their tears are like the gentle dew
Which brighten still that floweret's hue.

E'en if a cloud appears awhile
To dim their merry gleeful smile,
A rainbow will be planted there
In colours bright and passing fair.

And music dwells in childhood's voice
Which can the weary heart rejoice.

Its merry tones as blithely ring
As birds which welcome early spring.
                      [crowned
And joy that fair young head hath
As with a garland circling round,
Bright are the flowerets which compose
That wreath of joy untouched by woe.

But brightest of the blossoms there
And fairest of those flowerets fair,
That priceless gift from God above
In mercy sent: a mother's love.
                      [severed,
That flower from childhood's bosom
Its sweetest gift is gone for ever.
The wreath of joy! Oh how defaced!
How can <u>that</u> loss e'er be replaced.

Torn is that young and tender heart
When called from mother love to part.
Ah! manhood stern can never know
The depth of this its bitterest woe!

                      F.R.H. 1852

A mother's loss! Oh who may tell
Its anguish, or what power can quell
That deepest grief, most heartfelt woe
Which childhood's sunny hours may know

Ah! childhood's happy days are past
In mirth & glee; no shades are cast
Upon their bright & happy way
Where sunbeams e'er around them play.

No cares have they: the flow'ret sweet
Springs up to cheer their tiny feet
Their tears are like the gentle dew
Which brighten still that flow'rets hue.

E'en if a cloud appear awhile
To dim their merry, gleeful smile
A rainbow will be painted there
In colours bright & passing fair.

And music dwells in childhood's voice
Which can the weary heart rejoice.
Its merry tones as blithely ring
As birds which welcome early spring
And joy that fair young head hath crowned
As with a garland circling round
Bright are the flow'rets which compose
That wreath of joy untouched by woe.

But brightest of the blossoms there
And fairest of those flow'rets fair
That priceless gift from God above
In mercy sent; a Mother's love.

That flower from childhood's severed bosom
Its sweetest gift is gone for ever"

The wreath of joy! Oh how defaced!
How can that loss e'er be replaced.

Torn is that young & tender heart
When called from Mother love to part
Ah! manhood stern can never know
The depth of this its bitterest woe!

F. R. H.
April 1852

F.R.H.'s manuscript of "A mother's loss" on three sides of a single-fold sheet of paper. Frances was 15 in April, 1852. She was 11 when her mother died on July 5, 1848.

TRUST.

FIDES. [H. P. 343.]

569   Ps. lv. 23. *"I will trust in Thee."*
Tune FIDES. 65, 65. D.   Or HERMAS.

1 JESUS, I will trust Thee, trust Thee with my soul;
  Guilty, lost, and helpless, Thou canst make me whole.
There is none in heaven or on earth like Thee:
Thou hast died for sinners—therefore, Lord, for me.

2 Jesus, I may trust Thee, name of matchless
    worth
  Spoken by the angel at Thy wondrous birth;
Written, and for ever, on Thy cross of shame,
Sinners read and worship, trusting in that
    name.

3 Jesus, I must trust Thee, pondering Thy ways,
  Full of love and mercy all Thine earthly days:
Sinners gathered round Thee, lepers sought
    Thy face—
None too vile or loathsome for a Saviour's grace.

4 Jesus, I can trust Thee, trust Thy written word,
  Though Thy voice of pity I have never heard.
When Thy Spirit teacheth, to my taste how
    sweet—
Only may I hearken, sitting at Thy feet.

5 Jesus, I do trust Thee, trust without a doubt:
  "Whosoever cometh, Thou wilt not cast out,"
Faithful is Thy promise, precious is Thy blood—
These my soul's salvation, Thou my Saviour
    God!
                    Mary Jane Walker, 1864.

See *Hymns* 1076—1078.

* To this tune its composer, FRANCES RIDLEY HAVERGAL, sang the first verse of this hymn ten minutes only before her death, Tuesday morning, June 3, 1879.

HERMAS.*   [H. P. 105.]

570   1 Pet. v. 7. *"He careth for you."*
Tune SIHOR.   77, 77, 77.

1 QUIET, Lord, my froward heart,
    Make me teachable and mild,
  Upright, simple, free from art,
    Make me as a weanèd child,
  From distrust and envy free,
  Pleased with all that pleases Thee.

2 What Thou shalt to-day provide
    Let me as a child receive;
  What to-morrow may betide,
    Calmly to Thy wisdom leave:
  'Tis enough that Thou wilt care;
  Why should I the burden bear?

3 As a little child relies
    On a care beyond his own,
  Knows he's neither strong nor wise,
    Fears to stir a step alone,
  Let me thus with Thee abide,
  As my Father, Guard, and Guide.

4 Thus preserved from Satan's wiles,
    Safe from dangers, free from fears,
  May I live upon Thy smiles
    Till the promised hour appears,
  When the sons of God shall prove
  All their Father's boundless love!
                    John Newton, 1779.

See *Hymns* 99—103, 892.

SIHOR (River).   [H. P. 158.]

This is a page in Songs of Grace and Glory, *copied from the finalized "New and Enlarged Musical Edition" published in 1880, around six months after F. R. H. died. Read the asterisked note to the hymntune "Hermas" (the second tune for the hymn 569): "To this tune its composer, Frances Ridley Havergal, sang the first verse of this hymn ten minutes only before her death, Tuesday morning, June 3, 1879."*

These are a few poems by William Henry Havergal, F. R. H.'s father and a true servant of the Lord Jesus Christ. He was a pastor, a very fine musician, a scholar, and a poet.

The Holy Child.

"He was subject unto them."—Luke 2:51.

BLESSÈD Jesus, Lord and Brother,
   Once thou wast a lowly child,
Subject to Thy Virgin-mother,
   "Holy, harmless, undefiled;"
Wisdom, favour, grace, and truth,
Graced, like morning stars, Thy youth.

Great Redeemer, Mediator!
   Now Thou art enthroned in light;
But Thou wearest still our nature,
   And all heaven admires the sight.
Lord, to tender years impart
Mercy's boon, the tender heart.

Jesu, by Thy childhood's favour,
   By Thy manhood's agony,
Fill us with Thy Spirit's savour,
   Train us for eternity;
With the glittering hosts above,
May we sing Thy boundless love!

                                   1833.

The following acrostic by W. H. H. was copied by Mrs. Clement in 1858 when she was 86 (copied by Mrs. Clement for W.H.H.'s second wife, Mrs. Caroline A. Havergal), written decades earlier by W.H.H. for Mrs. Clement's son when he was a little boy. This is found in *Records of the Life of the Rev. William Henry Havergal* by Jane Miriam (Havergal) Crane (London: Home Words Publishing Office, 1882), Chapter 10. See page 644 of Volume IV of the Havergal edition.

D ear Jesus, teach a little child,
A nd kindly hear me when I pray;
V ouchsafe to me Thy mercy mild,
I nstruct me early in Thy way.
D raw, dearest Lord, my heart to Thee.

C leanse it from every youthful sin,
L et not the least impurity
E ntwine itself for ill within.
M ake me as David was when young,
E nriched by grace, beloved by Heaven;
N or let my heart, or hand, or tongue,
T ransgress the precepts Thou hast given.

Double Acrostic.

"A wise son maketh a glad father, but a foolish son is the heaviness of his mother."
—Proverbs 10:1

J oin to magnify and praise.	J	ointly, age and youth,
H im, the joy of all your days,	H	ear this standard truth!
S hall grace for grace confer.	S	ons who fathers gladden
H e who is the Saviour,	H	onours shall receive;
A ll who favour her;	A	ll who mothers sadden
W isdom loves to favour.	W	ill be sure to grieve.

For Miss Sarah Stenning.

I.

A nd its heavenly fragrancy!	A	s the blithe and busy bee
L ike its stainless purity,	L	oves to sip the honied flower,
B e your flowers of poesy	B	e each pen as choice as she,
U ndecaying as it grows;	U	nlocking with simplicity
M ark, then, friends, sweet Sharon's rose,	M	any a fair and balmy flower

1830.

II.

Double Acrostics by W.H.H.

To John Hall Shaw.

I.

S ons who fathers gladden,
H onours shall receive;
A ll who mothers sadden,
W ill be sure to grieve.

II.

W isdom loves to favour
A ll who favour her;
H e who is the Saviour
S hall grace for grace confer.

Langen Schwallbach, 1865.

To Miss Caroline Kingscote.

I.

K ind are thy gifts! and welcome as showers
I
N } opening spring to the delicate flowers,
G rowing most sweet by thy home's lovely bowers;
S o think my darlings and I.
C ould you but see their hearts in their faces,
O r witness their glee and their artless grimaces,
T } would gladden thy spirit when it retraces
E ven days that smiled once and went by.

II.

E ver, then, be thy lot simplicity's pleasure,
O
T } wisdom more dear than miserly treasure;
C ould but the world see its own empty measure,
S urely shame would soon tinge its proud cheek.
G o, go, worthless world! and curb thy vain spirit
N
I } or the lofty in heart, but the lowly inherit
    Jehovah's best gift, the robe of Christ's merit,
K ept for the childlike and meek.

1828.

Good Night.

Good night, good night!
Care take his flight,
And Peace, all bright,
Possess thee quite,
Through Christ our Light!
Good night, good night!

Good Morning.

Good morn, good morn, good morning!
  Be many a smile to-day!
May we, the truth adorning,
  Pass safely on our way.
When sin's fell thorn made us forlorn,
Christ came one morn, and joy was born.
Blest morn, blest morn, blest morning!
Good morn, good morn, good morning!

Grace before and after Meat.[1]

I.

No earthly gifts can yield us good,
Without, O Lord, Thy heavenly grace;
Then sanctify our present food,
And lift on us a Father's face.

II.

All praise to Him Who died to give
The Bread by which the dying live;
Our praise for all things pure shall be,
When face to face Himself we see.

I.

Jesus, Lord of earth and sky,
What Thou givest sanctify;

---

[1] "Meat" here (and also in earlier times before the 19th century) meant "food."

Always let our souls be fed
With Thyself, the living Bread.

II.

Jesus, seated on Thy throne,
Thee we bless and Thee alone;
Thee we bless for food and friends,
Every gift Thy mercy sends.

Coleridge, 1867.

Grace before Meat.

THOU, gracious Father, dost provide
All blessings in the Crucified;
What now Thou givest, sanctify,
And make us meet to feast on high.

Grace after Meat.

ALL praise to Him Who food supplies,
Through Christ's atoning sacrifice!
For gifts received our hymn we raise,
And hope to join in endless praise.

Penzance, October, 1868.

To Ellen, on her Third Birthday. [1]

19th February 1826.

COME, my pretty little love,
Sweet and harmless as the dove;
You, my February Queen,
Paper-crowned, with pink and green,
Happy, happy may you be
Often as this day you see!
Onward as through life you go,
May the Bible you well know!

---

[1] Ellen Prestage (Havergal) Shaw, his third daughter.

And when days and years are fled,
And you sleep among the dead,
May your spirit happy be
With the Great and Holy Three,
Clad in robes of holiness,
Crowned with everlasting bliss!

For Evelyn, Constance, and John Crane.[1]

CHILDREN, while you gather flowers,
Think how fleeting are your hours;
Think again in heavenly bowers,
You may cull unfading flowers.

Jesus is the sweetest flower:
Give to Him each passing hour,
He will then in Eden's bower
Make you each a fadeless flower.

[1] Three grandchildren, by his eldest daughter, Jane Miriam (Havergal) Crane. June, 1858.

Five Poems Hand-written in *The Christian Almanack for the Year 1842*

A little dialogue.

Francis! can you tell me why
The LORD JESUS came to die?

Oh yes, I can — for our sin came.
And have blessed is HIS Name.

Francis! have you learned to know
What to return to HIM, you owe?

Yes, I to HIM, my heart should give,
And love and serve HIM while I live.

Francis! will HE you receive,
If you on HIS Name believe?

Oh yes, boundless is HIS grace,
And I humbly early seek HIS face.

Francis! ask HIS mercy now
That your heart — to HIM may bow?

"Hear me, hear me, Lord. Divine,
"Take, will now, for ever THINE!

"I'm a little pilgrim.
"And a stranger here.
"Though this world is pleasant
"Sin is always near.

"Mine is a better country.
"Where there is no sin,
"Where the voices of sinner
"never enter in.

"But a little pilgrim
"Must have garments clean;
"If he'd wear the white robes,
"that with CHRIST be seen.

"LORD JESUS, Thou dost cleanse me,
"Teach me to obey;
"HOLY SPIRIT guide me,
"On my heavenly way.

"I'm a little pilgrim
"And a stranger here,
"But my HOME in HEAVEN
"Is in the ever near."

— Psalm 1
— Isaiah B. Exlvii
— Rev. iii
— xix
— xx/1   Revelation
— xi   Hebrews
No. 21

See pages 148–149.

Addendum

Hand-written Items in *The Christian Almanack for the Year 1842* found in papers of F. R. H. and her family.

Among Havergal manuscripts and papers was found *The Christian Almanack for the Year 1842*, a book published by the Religious Tract Society, London. The hand-written poems in this Almanack were very likely—or almost surely—written to or copied for Frances Ridley Havergal. (The next oldest child in the family was Francis Tebbs Havergal, whose 13th birthday was August 7, 1842.) The first and last poems have the author's name, Miss Threlfall and Emma Tasham; the other poems have no name for the author. The Scripture references at the end of the stanzas in the fifth poem ("I'm a little pilgrim") were copied as they were in the original book. These poems may have been written or copied by her mother, Jane Head Havergal, her father, William Henry Havergal, her oldest sister, Miriam, or by another: we do not know. Frances was five years old, becoming six on December 14, 1842.

Dear child! thy mother hath not
    A holier prayer for thee
Than that the lamb-like spirit
    Of Christ may be in thee.
Then carried to His bosom
    It shall be thine to share
In every time of danger
    A Shepherd's tender care.

And ever, like the daisy,
    Look up in sun and shower;
For none shall ever pluck thee
    From His almighty power,
Till, higher than the sky lark,
    Borne upon angel's wing,
It shall be thine to enter
    The city of our King.

                            Miss Threlfall.

Five Poems Hand-written in *The Christian Almanack for the Year 1842*

Mark 10:14

When Jesus dwelt upon this earth,
    His actions all were love;
He little children bless'd, and called
    Them to His house above.

Suffer them all to come to Me,
    Forbid them not, He cried;
For such My kingdom is prepared;
    For each of them I died.

What kind compassion must have beamed
    In His majestic eye,
While thus He welcomed them to reign
    With Him above the sky!

And still He little children loves,
    Tho' now He dwells in heaven;
Invites them to believe in Him,
    And have their sins forgiven.

Though now they cannot hear His voice
    Their hearts with joy to fill,
Yet little children may rejoice,
    For Jesus loves them still.

There is a book which He has given
    That tells them of His love;
He came from heaven their souls to save
    That they might dwell above.

Then, children, love that Saviour dear,
    And serve Him every day,
That hence you may behold His face
    For ever and for aye.

Hymn.

I am but a little child,
Very sinful, very wild,

And my heart will oft rebel,
Yet I love my Saviour well.

Yes, I love Him, who for me
Died upon th' accursed tree,
Died to save my soul from hell,
Yes, I love my Saviour well.

Sin defiles me, but I know
He can wash me white as snow;
I shall live where angels dwell,
If I love my Saviour well.

Blessed Lord, from all alarms
Fold thy lamb within Thine arms;
That my life and death may tell
That I love my Saviour well.

A little dialogue.

Francie! can you tell me why
The LORD JESUS came to die?

Oh yes, I can—for me HE came;
And how blessed is HIS name.

Francie! have you learned to know
What return to HIM you owe?

Yes, I to HIM my heart should give,
And love and serve HIM while I live.

Francie! will HE you receive
If you on HIS name believe?

Oh yes, boundless is HIS grace,
And I would early seek HIS face.

Francie! ask HIS mercy now,
That your heart to HIM may bow?

Hear me, hear me, Lamb Divine,
Make <u>me</u> <u>now</u> for <u>ever</u> <u>THINE</u>!

I'm a little pilgrim
And a stranger here,
Though this world is pleasant,
Sin is always near. Hebrews 11

Mine's a better country,
Where there is no sin,
Where the tones of sorrow
Never enter in. Revelation 21

But a little pilgrim
Must have garments clean,
If he'd wear the white robes,
And with CHRIST be seen. Revelation 3 & 19
　　　　　　　　　　　　　Psalm 51

LORD JESUS, save and cleanse me,
Teach me to obey;
HOLY SPIRIT, guide me,
On my heavenly way. 1 John 1
　　　　　　　　　　Psalm 143

I'm a little pilgrim
And a stranger here,
But my HOME in HEAVEN
Cometh ever near. John 14

　　　　　To little children.

There is a dove that from the glorious land
Flew on the wings of pity to this world,
To bring us a green branch from the tree
Of everlasting life, and if ye pray
That He will come and touch you with His breath,
How shall your heartstrings echo to the songs
I sing to you this day!
Listen then—your warm hearts are made to love.
All things are made to love us, we to love
All things. Is it not sweet? The little flowers
Are made to smile upon us, and the winds

To fan us, and the bright, hot sun, to paint
The flowers, the clouds, the rainbow and to warm
The winds, and fill our hearts and eyes with joy.
The stars are made to shine, the birds to sing,
The moon to smile, the trees to shade and shake
Sweet music out—not for themselves, but us.
The rain is made to fill the thirsty ground,
The rainbow tells God's beauty and His truth,
The storm His strength, the sea His majesty,
The grass His tenderness Who carpets thus
The earth for little lambs, and flowers, and us.
All things in this fair world for us are made
Except ourselves, and we are made for God,
To live and love like Him. Therefore, dear ones,
Learn what to love—not your own selves. Unfold
Your bosoms to the bliss of boundless love,
Like mirrors to the light, drops to the sun.
Look at the face of thy fond mother friend,
O darling child! look, what is that which shines
Out of her eyes? and what is that which lives
Upon her lips? and what is that which makes
Her bosom such a warm nest for thy head?
And what is that which folds and holds around thee
Her gentle arms so tight and tenderly?
My darling, it is love. Then thou must try
To shew her how it charms thee; do thou smile
When she is smiling,—kiss away her tears
When she is weeping,—do thou clap thy hands
When she is singing to thee, and at night
Sleep on her bosom without tear or fear.
Love thou each soothing voice that circles thee,
Each kindly face that woos thee, love thou all
And everything around thee; love the flowers,
For they love thee; love the sun to warm,
That shines upon thee, love the rainbow fair,
The glorious ocean, and the drops of dew
Gladdening the thirsty roses; love the winds,
The storms, the lightnings, and the gorgeous clouds.
Stretch thy baby hands to the great things

Which God hath set to serve thee, the broad skies,
The stars, the tempests,—greet them with a kiss
And song of love; fear thou not anything,
Redeemed, God-belovèd, deathless soul;
But love thou all, and let the robe of love
Enwrap thee as thou walkest through the world;
Love thou the birds, the bees, the butterflies,
And all things that have life.
                      But One there is
Whom, though thou canst not see, yet thou must love
More than aught else. He gave thee this warm life
Which dances through thy senses, the young flame
Of immortality which fires thy breast.
He gave thee thy sweet father, mother, sister,
He gave thee the bright sun, flowers, trees,
The stars, the winds, the thunder and the moon.
He holds thee in His arms, He every night
Watches thee in thy slumbers. He did once
For love of thee forsake the beauteous land.
                      He was a Babe
As lowly as thyself; He wept and died
That thou shouldst love Him, and that He might be
Thy Saviour, and that thou should'st never die.
Oh, my fair darling, if thou live to know
The friendship of the world, then thou wilt find
Thy love neglected, and thy aching heart
Pierced with a thousand sorrows, left alone
To agonize to death. But ere that hour
Seek refuge in the ark of God, sweet dove.
Thou may'st pour out thy first fresh tears to Him,
Thou may'st reveal thy every joy and grief
Before His gentle presence. He is here
And everywhere; He sees thine every thought,
He hears thine every word, and His dear name
Is Love. Once did He come and lowly tread
This same green world of ours, and then He blessed
The little children, and His name was called
Our Saviour Jesus Christ. There is no one
Loves you so much as He does; He has wept

Tears for your tears; has shed His own blood out
That you might live; and now He ever looks
And loves you. He is very fair and far
More beautiful than all: more bright and clear
Than the great sun, more mighty and more strong
Than sea or wind or thunder; and more fair
Than lily of the valley, sweeter far
Than June's first red rose; and more high and pure
Than the bright stars; more lovely than the light,
And kinder than thy mother; and His name
Is Love. Oh, darling, darling little ones!
I bring you unto Him, that He may lay
His piercèd hands alike on you and me,
And breathe into our bosoms the same life
And love which fill His own.

From "The Dream of Pythagoras and Other Poems."
Emma Tasham.

This next hymn was found in *God Is Love; or, Memorials of Little Nony*, a small book published in Volume IV of this Havergal edition. The author is not known, likely not F. R. H.

I.

Lord, look upon a little child,
By nature sinful, rude, and wild;
Oh! put Thy gracious hands on me,
And make me all I ought to be.

II.

Make me Thy child, a child of God,
Washed in my Saviour's precious blood;
And my whole heart from sin set free,
A little vessel full of Thee.

III.

A star of early dawn, and bright,
Shining within Thy sacred light;
A beam of light to all around,
A little spot of hallowed ground.

IV.

Dear Jesus, take me to Thy breast,
And bless me that I may be blest;
Both when I wake and when I sleep,
Thy little lamb in safety keep.

Richard Wilton (1827–1903) was a pastor, scholar, poet, and friend whom F.R.H. knew. He had a special gift, to be able to win over and gently hold timid, wild creatures. Bluey was a rabbit in Scotland that Wilton brought to live in his home in England. What he describes here is real, and the truth he presents here is so valuable.

A Lesson of Trust.

I learn to trust from this dear Highland Hare,
   Which lays its gentle head upon my arm,
   And dozes on my knee without alarm,
As if it slumbered in its native lair.
Far from its heathery home and mountain air—
   How comes it that it never dreams of harm?
   What has subdued its fear? What potent charm
Commands this confidence so sweet and rare?
Love, true and constant, is the only spell;
   Kindness of act and feeling, voice and eye,
Has won its timorous heart to trust me well:
   Nor will I doubt my Benefactor high,
Whose kindnesses are more than I can tell,
   But trustful on His loving arm will lie.

Richard Wilton

Singing for Jesus.

Singing for Jesus, our Saviour & King,
Singing for Jesus, the Lord whom we love!
All adoration we joyously bring,
Longing to praise as they praise Him above.

Singing for Jesus, our Master & Friend,
Telling His love & His marvellous grace,
Love from eternity, love without end,
Love for the loveless, the sinful, & base.

Singing for Jesus, and trying to win
Many to love Him & join in the song;
Calling the weary and wandering in,
Rolling the chorus of gladness along.

Singing for Jesus, our Life & our Light,
Singing for Him as we press to the mark;
Singing for Him when the morning is bright,
Singing, still singing, for Him in the dark!

Singing for Jesus, our Shepherd & Guide,
Singing for gladness of heart that He gives;
Singing for wonder & praise that He died,
Singing for blessing & joy that He lives.

Singing for Jesus, oh singing with joy!
Thus will we praise Him, & tell out His love,
Till He shall call us to brighter employ,
Singing for Jesus for ever above.

June 12.

A poem in F.R.H.'s Manuscript Book Nº VI, written June 12, 1872.

Index to First Lines of Poems.

	PAGE(S)
A bright and joyous frame of mind	.115
A few months ago I was singing through the snow	. 7
A happy New Year! O such may it be!	. 23
A term for autumn leaves when all their lovely tints are fled	. 92
A whimsical set we must often seem	. 89
All praise to Him Who food supplies	.143
An army of Cyclops, fair reader, are we	. 89
Arise, my *first!* In peerless radiance beaming	.110
As the blithe and busy bee	.140
Awake, ye sleepers!	.110
Begin at once! In the pleasant day	. 22
Blessèd Jesus, Lord and Brother	.139
Blessings on thee, darling boy	. 37
Buds and bells! Sweet April pleasures	. 8
By Him "Life's *Morning*" lovelit be	.118
Children, while you gather flowers	.144
Come away, come away, in the dawn of May	. 27
Come, my pretty little love	.143
Darling boy, Sister's joy, With your loving smile	. 21
Dear child! thy mother hath not	.146
Dear Jesus, teach a little child	.140
Did I tell you how we went to tea	. 17
Distant from the noisy town	.108
Do the angels know the blessed day	. 31
Enter my *first* with a studied grace	.112
Every little flower that grows	. 20
Far off upon a western shore	. 64
Five-twelfths 5/12 of the square of 3/5 of a score	. 113, 88
Francie and Willie, welcome to you!	.119
Francie! can you tell me why	.148
From childish days I never heard	.130

From his ruby pavilion Phoebus arose	.105
God of heaven ! hear our singing	. 16
Golden harps are sounding.	. 28
Good morn, good morn, good morning!	.142
Good night, good night!	.142
He stood upon the fiery deck	. 56
Heard ye the long, low roar	.111
Here beginneth—chapter the first of a series	. 53
Hurrah for merry England!	.105
I am a native of many a land	. 90
I am a reward, and a punishment too.	. 95
I am but a little child .	.147
I am the child of the brightest thing	.100
I learn to trust from this dear Highland Hare	.153
I may be tall, and slender, and round .	. 97
"I thought I knew it!" she said	. 51
If you get into me, I have no sort of doubt.	. 93
In fiery caverns was my glowing birth.	. 94
It was Easter Monday morning .	. 69
Jesus, blessèd Saviour, Help us now to raise	. 24
Jesus, I will trust Thee, trust Thee with my soul .	.138
Jointly, age and youth, Hear this standard truth .	.140
Kind are thy gifts ! and welcome as showers	.141
Knowing that the God on high .	. 51
Leaning over the waterfall !	. 55
Little Jessie, darling pet, Do you want a Friend .	. 70
Little one, what are you doing	.127
Lives there a poet, old or young .	. 96
Lord, I am in Thy house of prayer	. 15
Lord, in mercy pardon me .	. 14
Lord, look upon a little child	.152
May the tale the years are telling	. 34
My *first* dwells in the torrid zone	.109
My *first* gleams bright 'mid azure shields	.104
My *first* had spread her darksome wing	.110
My lodging was on the cold rough ground.	.125
My second could never produce my first	.106
My whole is but a species of my third.	.111
My whole, the poet of flood and fell .	.108

Index to First Lines of Poems

No earthly gifts can yield us good	.142
Not long ago the moon was dark	. 10
Now let us sing the Angels' Song	. 30
Now the light has gone away	. 15
O haste, O haste to the fields away!	. 26
O sweet Sabbath bells!	. 13
O Thou who gatherest with loving arm	.117
Of a useful *whole* I'm the most useful part	. 91
Oh, children of England, beyond the blue sea	. 67
Oh God, with grateful hearts we come	.132
Oh, haughty Thebes! In shadowy days of yore	.103
Oh, must we not sing our Christmas hymn	.118
Once on a time I a visit had paid	.120
Only just a line to say.	. 37
Out in the midsummer sunshine	. 40
Primeval woods my parent's birth	.100
Read to him, Connie, read as you sit	. 42
Sadly bend the flowers In the heavy rain	. 13
Say, is not my whole a prize	.115
Say, know ye not the pilgrim band	.102
Seventeen hundred and sixty yards	. 92
Shall those who name the name of Christ (in "A Plea for the Little Ones").	. 72
She stood by the western window	. 73
So it has come to you, dear	. 57
"Something to do, mamma, something to do!"	. 59
Sons who fathers gladden, honours shall receive.	.141
Soon the hour of dawn shall pass	.108
Sweet flowers of Spring, All fresh and fair to see.	.118
Sybil, my little one, come away	. 29
That I'm very well-known to all metaphysicians 'tis true	. 97
The all-victorious Roman	.112
The golden gates were opening	. 49
The golden glow is paling	. 11
The lessons are done and the prizes won	. 47
The Lord is gracious—full of grace	.133
The royal sun with his orbèd flame	. 94
The Sabbath morn dawns o'er the mountain brow	. 45
The Severn flow is soft and fair, as slowly	. 44

The stars die out, and the moon grows dim	77
The sun is burning, O little maiden	44
The Sunbeams came to my window	39
The veiling shades of night departed	104
There is a dove that from the glorious land.	149
They said their texts, and their hymns they sang.	16
They tell me that my little tree	9
Thou, gracious Father, dost provide	143
Though constantly we're in the mire	103
Tiny feet so busy in a tiny patter out of sight	43
We have heard the call from your fair green Isle	68
What do we seek for him to-day, who, through such golden gates	39
What was I? Such a clever friar	93
"What wouldst thou be?"	125
When Jesus dwelt upon this earth	147
Where the tall pine-forest made	107
Where will ye seek me? The Andes rise	98
"Who will take care of me?" darling, you say!	12
Will you come out and see My pretty bower with me.	10
Ye have seen me in the skies	101
Yes, take the greenery away.	25

"Stay and Think" — also named "Love for Love"

STAY AND THINK.

Words and Music by
Frances Ridley Havergal

1. Knowing that the God on high, With a tender Father's grace, Waits to hear your faintest cry, Waits to show a Father's face:— Stay and Think! Stay and Think! Stay and Think! Stay and Think! How He loves! Oh, should not you Love this gracious Father too?

2. Knowing Christ was crucified,
   Knowing that He loves you now
  Just as much as when He died
   With the thorns upon His brow,—
  Stay and think! — oh, should not you
  Love this blessèd Saviour too?

3. Knowing that a Spirit strives
   With your weary, wandering heart,
  Who can change the restless lives,
   Pure and perfect peace impart,—
  Stay and think! — oh, should not you
  Love this loving Spirit too?

To Thee.

'Lord, to whom shall we go?'—John 6:68.

I BRING my sins to Thee,
    The sins I cannot count,
That all may cleansèd be
    In Thy once opened Fount.
I bring them, Saviour, all to Thee,
The burden is too great for me.

My heart to Thee I bring,
    The heart I cannot read;
A faithless, wandering thing,
    An evil heart indeed.
I bring it, Saviour, now to Thee,
That fixed and faithful it may be.

To Thee I bring my care,
    The care I cannot flee;
Thou wilt not only share,
    But bear it all for me.
O loving Saviour, now to Thee
I bring the load that wearies me.

I bring my grief to Thee,
    The grief I cannot tell;
No words shall needed be,
    Thou knowest all so well.
I bring the sorrow laid on me,
O suffering Saviour, now to Thee.

My joys to Thee I bring,
    The joys Thy love hath given,
That each may be a wing
    To lift me nearer heaven.
I bring them, Saviour, all to Thee,
For Thou hast purchased all for me.

My life I bring to Thee,
    I would not be my own;
O Saviour, let me be
    Thine ever, Thine alone.
My heart, my life, my all I bring
To Thee, my Saviour and my King!

                      Frances Ridley Havergal

www.ingramcontent.com/pod-product-compliance
Lightning Source LLC
Chambersburg PA
CBHW071505040426
42444CB00008B/1504